Granville Barker's
Prefaces to Shakespeare

JULIUS CAESAR

Foreword by
Richard Eyre

NICK HERN BOOKS

First published in this collected paperback edition in 1993 jointly by
Nick Hern Books Limited, 14 Larden Road, London W3 7ST
and the Royal National Theatre, London,
by arrangement with Batsford.

Preface to Julius Caesar. Originally published in 1925, revised 1927

Set in 10/11 Baskerville by Pure Tech Corporation, Pondicherry
(India)
Printed in Australia by
Australian Print Group

A CIP catalogue record for this book is available from the British
Library

ISBN 1 85459 113 4

Shakespeare Alive!

The history of the theatre in England in this century can be told largely through the lives and work of two men: George Bernard Shaw and Harley Granville Barker, a triple-barrelled cadence of names that resonates like the ruffling of the pages of a large book in a silent public library. One was a brilliant polemicist who dealt with certainties and assertions and sometimes, but not often enough, breathed life into his sermons; the other a committed sceptic who started from the premise that the only thing certain about human behaviour was that nothing was certain. Both, however, possessed a passionate certainty about the importance of the theatre and the need to revise its form, its content, and the way that it was managed. Shaw was a playwright, critic and pamphleteer, Barker a playwright, director and actor.

The Voysey Inheritance is, at least in my opinion, Granville Barker's best play: a complex web of family relationships, a fervent but never unambiguous indictment of a world dominated by the mutually dependent obsessions of greed, class, and self-deception. It's also a virtuoso display of stagecraft: the writer showing that as director he can handle twelve speaking characters on stage at one time, and that as actor he can deal with the most ambitious and unexpected modulations of thought and feeling. The 'inheritance' of the Voyseys is a legacy of debt, bad faith, and bitter family dissension. Edward's father has, shortly before his death, revealed that he has been cheating the family firm of solicitors for many years, as his father had for many years before that. Towards the end of the play Edward Voysey, the youngest son, confronts the woman he loves:

iv

> EDWARD. Why wouldn't he own the truth to me about himself?
>
> BEATRICE. Perhaps he took care not to know it. Would you have understood?
>
> EDWARD. Perhaps not. But I loved him.
>
> BEATRICE. That would silence a bench of judges.

Shaw would have used the story to moralise and polemicise. He might have had the son hate the father; he might have had him forgive him; he might have had him indict him as a paradigm of capitalism; he would never have said he loved him.

Everybody needs a father, or, failing that, a father-figure. He may be a teacher, a prophet, a boss, a priest perhaps, a political leader, a friend, or, sometimes, if you are very lucky, the real one. If you can't find a father you must invent him. In some ways, not altogether trivial, Granville Barker is something of a father-figure for me. He's a writer whom I admire more than any twentieth-century English writer before the sixties – Chekhov with an English accent; he's the first modern British director; he's the real founder of the National Theatre and, in his *Prefaces*, he's a man who, alone amongst Shakespearean commentators before Jan Kott, believed in the power of Shakespeare on stage.

There was a myth that Granville Barker was the natural son of Shaw. He was certainly someone whom Shaw could, in his awkward way, cherish and admire, educate and castigate. When Barker fell wildly in love ('in the Italian manner' as Shaw said) with Helen Huntington, an American millionairess, he married her, acquired a hyphen in his surname, moved first to Devon to play the part of a country squire, and then to France to a life of seclusion. Shaw thought that he had buried himself alive and could never reconcile himself to the loss. It was, as his biographer

Hesketh Pearson said: 'The only important matter about which he asked me to be reticent.'

After directing many of Shaw's plays for many years, acting many of his best roles (written by Shaw with Barker in mind), dreaming and planning together the birth of a National Theatre, not to mention writing, directing, and acting in his own plays while managing his own company at the Royal Court, Barker withdrew from the theatre, and for twenty years there was silence between the two men. Only on the occasion of the death of Shaw's wife did they communicate by letters. 'I did not know I could be so moved by anything,' wrote Shaw to him.

Out of this self-exile came one major work, slowly assembled over many years: *The Prefaces to Shakespeare*. With a few exceptions (Auden on *Othello*, Barbara Everett on *Hamlet*, Jan Kott on *The Tempest*) it's the only critical work about Shakespeare that's made any impact on me, apart, that is, from my father's view of Shakespeare, which was brief and brutal: 'It's absolute balls.'

As much as we need a good father, we need a good teacher. Mine, improbably perhaps, was Kingsley Amis. He'd arrived, somewhat diffidently, at Cambridge at the same time as I did. The depth of my ignorance of English literature corresponded almost exactly to his dislike of the theatre. Nevertheless, he made me see Shakespeare with a mind uncontaminated by the views of academics, whom he would never have described as his fellows and whose views he regarded as, well, academic. I would write essays marinated in the opinions of Spurgeon, Wilson Knight, Dover Wilson and a large cast of critical supernumeraries. He would gently, but courteously, cast aside my essay about, say, *Twelfth Night*: 'But what do *you* think of this play? Do you think it's any good?' 'Well ... er ... it's Shakespeare.' 'Yes, but is it any *good*? I mean as a *play*. It says it's a comedy. Fine. But does it have any decent jokes?'

I took this for irreverence, heresy even. Over the years, however, I've come to regard this as good teaching, or, closely allied, good direction. It's asking the right questions, unintimidated by reputation, by tradition, by received opinion, or by critical orthodoxy. This was shocking, but healthy, for a young and impressionable man ripe to become a fundamentalist in matters of literary taste and ready to revere F. R. Leavis as the Ayatollah of 'Cambridge English'. What you have is yourself and the text, only that. That's the lesson of Granville Barker: 'We have the text to guide us, half a dozen stage directions, and that is all. I abide by the text and the demands of the text and beyond that I claim freedom.' I can't imagine a more useful and more enduring dictum.

The Prefaces have a practical aim: 'I want to see Shakespeare made fully effective on the English stage. That is the best sort of help I can lend.' What Granville Barker wrote is a primer for directors and actors working on the plays of Shakespeare. There is lamentably little useful literature about the making of theatre, even though there is an indigestible glut of memoirs and biographies, largely concerned with events that have taken place *after* the curtain has fallen. If I was asked by a visiting Martian to recommend books which would help him, her or it to make theatre in the manner of the European I could only offer four books: Stanislavsky on *The Art of the Stage*, John Willett's *Brecht on Theatre*, Peter Brook's *The Empty Space*, and *The Prefaces to Shakespeare*.

Stanislavsky offers a pseudo-scientific dissection of the art of acting which is, in some respects, like reading Freud on the mechanism of the joke: earnest, well-meaning, but devoid of the indispensable ingredient of its subject matter: humour. Stanislavsky's great contribution was to demand that actors hold the mirror up to nature, that they take their craft as seriously as the writers they served, and to provide some sort of formal discipline within which both aims could be realised.

Brecht provided a manifesto that was a political and aesthetic response to the baroque encrustations of the scenery-laden, star-dominated, archaic boulevard theatre of Germany in the twenties. Although much of what he wrote as theory is an unpalatable mix of political ideology and artistic instruction, it is his theatrical instinct that prevails. He asserts, he insists, he browbeats. He demands that the stage, like society, must be re-examined, reformed, that the audience's habits mustn't be satisfied, they must be changed, but just when he is about to nail his 13 Articles to the church door he drops the voice of the zealot: 'The stage is not a hothouse or a zoological museum full of stuffed animals. It must be peopled with live, three-dimensional self-contradictory people with their passions, unconsidered utterances and actions.' In all art forms, he says, the guardians of orthodoxy will assert that there are eternal and immutable laws that you ignore at your peril, but in the theatre there is only one inflexible rule: 'The proof of the pudding is in the eating.' Brecht teaches us to ask the question: what goes on in a theatre?

Brook takes that question even further: what *is* theatre? It's a philosophical, but eminently practical, question that Brook has been asking for over 30 years and which has taken him to the African desert, a quarry in Iran, and an abandoned music hall in Paris. 'I take an empty space and call it a bare stage. A man walks across this empty space while someone else is watching him, and that is all that is needed for an act of theatre to be engaged.' For all his apparent concern with metaphyics, there is no more practical man of the theatre than Brook.

I was once at a seminar where someone asked him what was the job of the director. 'To get the actors on and off stage,' he said. Like Brecht, like Stanislavsky, like Granville Barker, Brook argues that for the theatre to be expressive it must be, above all, simple and unaffected: a distillation of language, of gesture, of action, of design, where meaning is the essence. The meaning must be felt as much as understood. 'They don't have to understand with their ears,' says Granville Barker, 'just with their guts.'

Brecht did not acknowledge a debt to Granville Barker. Perhaps he was not aware of one, but it seems to me that Barker's Shakespeare productions were the direct antecedents of Brecht's work. He certainly knew enough about English theatre to know that he was on to a good thing adapting *The Beggar's Opera*, *The Recruiting Officer* and *Coriolanus*. Brecht has been lauded for destroying illusionism; Granville Barker has been unhymned. He aimed at re-establishing the relationship between actor and audience that had existed in Shakespeare's theatre – and this at a time when the prevailing style of Shakespearean production involved *not* stopping short of having live sheep in *As You Like It*. He abolished footlights and the proscenium arch, building out an apron over the orchestra pit which Shaw said 'apparently trebled the spaciousness of the stage. . . . To the imagination it looks as if he had invented a new heaven and a new earth.'

His response to staging Shakespeare was not to look for a synthetic Elizabethanism. 'We shall not save our souls by being Elizabethan.' To recreate the Globe would, he knew, be aesthetic anasthaesia, involving the audience in an insincere conspiracy to pretend that they were willing collaborators in a vain effort to turn the clock back. His answers to staging Shakespeare were similar to Brecht's for *his* plays and, in some senses, to

Chekhov's for his. He wanted scenery not to decorate and be literal, but to be expressive and metaphorical, and at the same time, in apparent contradiction, to be specific and be real, while being minimal and iconographic: the cart in *Mother Courage*, the nursery in *The Cherry Orchard*, the dining table in *The Voysey Inheritance*. 'To create a new hieroglyphic language of scenery. That, in a phrase, is the problem. If the designer finds himself competing with the actors, the sole interpreters Shakespeare has licensed, then it is he that is the intruder and must retire.'

In *The Prefaces* Granville Barker argues for a fluency of staging unbroken by scene changes. Likewise the verse should be spoken fast. 'Be swift, be swift, be not poetical,' he wrote on the dressing-room mirror of Cathleen Nesbitt when she played Perdita. Within the speed, however, detailed reality. *Meaning* above all.

It is the director's task, with the actors, to illuminate the meanings of a play: its vocabulary, its syntax, and its philosophy. The director has to ask what each scene is revealing about the characters and their actions: what story is each scene telling us? In *The Prefaces* Granville Barker exhumes, examines and explains the lost stagecraft of Shakespeare line by line, scene by scene, play by play.

Directing Shakespeare is a matter of understanding the meaning of a scene and staging it in the light of that knowledge. Easier said than done, but it's at the heart of the business of directing any play, and directing Shakespeare is merely directing writ large. Beyond that, as David Mamet has observed, 'choice of actions and adverbs constitute the craft of directing'. Get up from that chair and walk across the room. Slowly.

With Shakespeare as with any other playwright the director's job is to make the play live, now, in the present

x

tense. 'Spontaneous enjoyment is the life of the theatre,'
says Granville Barker in his Preface to *Love's Labour's
Lost*. To receive a review, as Granville Barker did, headed
SHAKESPEARE ALIVE! is the most, but should be the
least, that a director must hope for.

I regard Granville Barker not only as the first modern
English director but as the most influential. Curiously,
partly as a result of his early withdrawal from the
theatre, partly because his *Prefaces* have been out of print
for many years, and partly because of his own
self-effacement, he has been unjustly ignored both in
the theatre and in the academic world, where
the codification of their 'systems' has resulted in the
canonisation of Brecht and Stanislavsky. I hope the
re-publication of *The Prefaces* will right the balance.
Granville Barker himself always thought of them as his
permanent legacy to the theatre.

My sense of filial identification is not entirely a
professional one. When I directed *The Voysey Inheritance* I
wanted a photograph of the author on the poster. A
number of people protested that it was the height, or
depth, of vanity and self-aggrandisement to put my own
photograph on the poster. I was astonished, I was
bewildered, but I was not unflattered. I still can't see the
resemblance, but it's not through lack of trying.

Two years ago the Royal National Theatre was
presented with a wonderful bronze bust of Granville
Barker by Katherine Scott (the wife, incidentally, of the
Antarctic hero). For a while it sat on the windowsill of
my office like a benign household god. Then it was
installed on a bracket in the foyer opposite a bust of
Olivier, the two men eyeing each other in wary mutual
regard. A few months later it was stolen; an act of
homage perhaps. I miss him.

Richard Eyre

Introduction

We have still much to learn about Shakespeare the playwright. Strange that it should be so, after three centuries of commentary and performance, but explicable. For the Procrustean methods of a changed theatre deformed the plays, and put the art of them to confusion; and scholars, with this much excuse, have been apt to divorce their Shakespeare from the theatre altogether, to think him a poet whose use of the stage was quite incidental, whose glory had small relation to it, for whose lapses it was to blame.

The Study and the Stage

THIS much is to be said for Garrick and his predecessors and successors in the practice of reshaping Shakespeare's work to the theatre of their time. The essence of it was living drama to them, and they meant to keep it alive for their public. They wanted to avoid whatever would provoke question and so check that spontaneity of response upon which acted drama depends. Garrick saw the plays, with their lack of 'art', through the spectacles of contemporary culture; and the bare Elizabethan stage, if it met his mind's eye at all, doubtless as a barbarous makeshift. Shakespeare was for him a problem; he tackled it, from our point of view, misguidedly and with an overplus of enthusiasm. His was a positive world; too near in time, moreover, as well as too opposed in taste to Shakespeare's to treat it perspectively. The romantic movement might have brought a more concordant outlook. But by then the scholars were off their own way; while the theatre began to think of its Shakespeare from the point of view of the picturesque, and, later, in terms of upholstery. Nineteenth-century drama developed along the lines of realistic illusion, and the staging of Shakespeare was further subdued to this, with inevitably disastrous effect on the speaking of his verse; there was less perversion of text perhaps, but actually more wrenching of the construction of the plays for the convenience of the stage carpenter. The public appetite for this sort of thing having been gorged, producers then turned to newer—and older—contrivances, leaving 're-alism' (so called) to the modern comedy that had fathered it. Amid much vaporous theorizing—but let us humbly own how hard it is not to write nonsense about art, which seems ever pleading to be enjoyed and not written about at all—the surprising discovery had been made that varieties of stagecraft and stage were not historical accidents but artistic obligations, that Greek drama belonged in a Greek theatre, that Elizabethan plays, therefore, would, presumably, do best upon an Elizabethan stage, that there was nothing sacrosanct about scenery, footlights, drop-curtain or any of their belongings. This brings us to the present situation.

There are few enough Greek theatres in which Greek tragedy can be played; few enough people want to see it, and they will applaud it encouragingly however it is done. Some acknowledgement is due to the altruism of the doers! Shakespeare is another matter. The English theatre, doubtful of its destiny, of necessity venal, opening its doors to all comers, seems yet, as by some instinct, to seek renewal of strength in him. An actor, unless success has made him cynical, or his talent be merely trivial, may take some pride in the hall mark of Shakespearean achievement. So may a manager if he thinks he can afford it. The public (or their spokesmen) seem to consider Shakespeare and his genius a sort of national property, which, truly, they do nothing to conserve, but in which they have moral rights not lightly to be flouted. The production of the plays is thus still apt to be marked by a timid respect for 'the usual thing'; their acting is crippled by pseudo-traditions, which are inert because they are not Shakespearean at all. They are the accumulation of two centuries of progressive misconception and distortion of his playwright's art. On the other hand, England has been spared production of Shakespeare according to this or that even more irrelevant theory of presentationalism, symbolism, constructivism or what not. There is the breach in the wall of 'realism', but we have not yet made up our minds to pass through, taking our Shakespeare with us.

Incidentally, we owe the beginning of the breach to Mr William Poel, who, with fanatical courage, when 'realism' was at the tottering height of its triumph in the later revivals of Sir Henry Irving, and the yet more richly upholstered revelations of Sir Herbert Tree, thrust the Elizabethan stage in all its apparent eccentricity upon our unwilling notice.[1] Mr Poel shook complacency. He could not expect to do much more; for he was a logical reformer. He showed us the Elizabethan stage, with Antony and Cleopatra, Troilus and Cressida, in their ruffs and farthingales as for Shakespeare's audiences they lived. Q.E.D. There, however, as far as the popular theatre was concerned, the matter seemed to rest for twenty years or so. But it was just such a demonstration that was needed; anything less drastic and provocative might have been passed over with mild approval.

To get the balance true, let us admit that while Shakespeare was an Elizabethan playwright he was—and now is to us—predominantly something much more. Therefore we had better not too unquestioningly thrust him back within the confines his genius has escaped, nor presume him to have felt the pettier circumstances of his theatre sacrosanct. Nor can we turn Elizabethans as we watch the plays; and every mental effort to do so will subtract from our enjoyment of them. This is the case against the circumstantial reproduction of Shakespeare's staging. But Mr Poel's achievement remains; he cleared for us from Shakespeare's stagecraft the scenic rubbish by which it had been so long encumbered and disguised. And we could now, if we would, make a promising fresh start. For the scholars, on their side, have lately—the scholarly among them—cut clear of the transcendental fog (scenic illusion of another sort) in which their nineteenth-century peers loved to lose themselves, and they too are beginning again at the beginning. A text acquires virtue now by its claim to be a prompt book, and the most comprehensive work of our time upon the Elizabethan stage is an elaborate sorting-out of plays, companies and theatres. On Dr Pollard's treatment of the texts and on the foundations of fact laid by Sir Edmund Chambers a new scholarship is rising, aiming first to see Shakespeare in the theatre for which he wrote. It is a scholarship, therefore, by which the theatre of today can profit, to which, by its acting of Shakespeare, it could contribute, one would hope. Nor should the scholars disdain the help; for criticism cannot live upon criticism, it needs refreshment from the living art. Besides, what is all the criticism and scholarship finally for if not to keep Shakespeare alive? And he must always be most alive—even if roughly and rudely alive—in the theatre. Let the scholars force a way in there, if need be. Its fervid atmosphere will do them good; the benefit will be mutual.

These Prefaces are an attempt to profit by this new scholarship and to contribute to it some research into Shakespeare's stagecraft, by examining the plays, one after another, in the light of the interpretation he designed for them, so far as this can be deduced; to discover, if possible, the production he would have desired for them, all merely incidental circumstances apart. They might profit more written a generation hence, for the ground they build upon is still far from clear. And this introduction is by no means a conspectus of the subject; that can only come as a sequel. There has been, in this branch of Shakespearean study, too much generalization and far too little analysis of material.[2]

Shakespeare's Stagecraft

SHAKESPEARE'S own career was not a long one. The whole history of the theatre he wrote for does not cover a century. Between Marlowe and Massinger, from the first blaze to the glowing of the embers, it is but fifty years. Yet even while Shakespeare was at work, the stage to which he fitted his plays underwent constant and perhaps radical change. From Burbage's first theatre to the Globe, then to Blackfriars, not to mention excursions to Court and into the great halls—change of audiences and their behaviour, of their taste, development of the art of acting, change of the stage itself and its resources were all involved in the progress, and are all, we may be sure, reflected to some degree in the plays themselves. We guess at the conditions of each sort of stage and theatre, but there is often the teasing question to which of them had a play, as we have it now, been adapted. And of the 'private' theatre, most in vogue for the ten years preceding the printing of the First Folio so far we know least. The dating of texts and their ascription to the usages of a particular theatre may often be a searchlight upon their stagecraft. Here is much work for the new scholarship.

Conversely, the watchful working-out of the plays in action upon this stage or that would be of use to the scholars, who otherwise must reconstruct their theatre and gloss their texts as in a vacuum. The play was once fitted to the stage; it is by no means impossible to rebuild that stage now, with its doors, balconies, curtains and machines, by measuring the needs of the play. It is idle, for instance, to imagine scenes upon inner or upper stage without evidence that they will be audible or visible there; and editing is still vitiated by lack of this simple knowledge. Here, if nowhere else, this present research must fall short, for its method should rightly be experimental; more than one mind should be at work on it, moreover.

The text of a play is a score waiting performance, and the performance and its preparation are, almost from the beginning, a work of collaboration. A producer may direct the preparation, certainly. But if he only knows how to give orders, he has mistaken his vocation; he had better be a drill-sergeant. He might talk to his company when they all met together for the first time to study *Love's Labour's Lost, Julius Cæsar* or *King Lear*, on some such lines as these Prefaces pursue, giving a considered opinion of the play, drawing a picture of it in action, providing, in fact, a hypothesis which mutual study would prove—and might partly disprove. No sort of study of a play can better the preparation of its performance if this is rightly done. The matured art of the playwright lies in giving life to characters in action, and the secret of it in giving each character a due chance in the battle, the action of a play becoming literally the fighting of a battle of character. So the greater the playwright, the wider and deeper his sympathies, the more genuine this opposition will be and the less easily will a single mind grasp it, as it must be grasped, in the fullness of its emotion. The dialogue of a play runs—and often intricately—upon lines of reason, but it is charged besides with an emotion which speech releases, yet only releases fully when the speaker is—as an actor is—identified with the character. There is further the incidental action, implicit in the dialogue, which springs to life only when a scene is in being. A play, in fact, as we find it written, is a magic spell; and even the magician cannot always foresee the full effect of it.

Not every play, it must be owned, will respond to such intensive study. Many, ambitiously conceived, would collapse under the strain. Many are mere occasions for display of their actors' wit or eloquence, good looks or nice behaviour, and meant to be no more; and if they are skilfully contrived the parts fit together and the whole machine should go like clockwork. Nor, in fact, are even the greatest plays often so studied. There is hardly a theatre in the world where masterpiece and trumpery alike are not rushed through rehearsals to an arbitrarily effective performance, little more learned of them than the words, gaps in the understanding of them filled up with 'business'—effect without cause, the demand for this being the curse of the theatre as of other arts, as of other things than art. Not to such treatment will the greater plays of Shakespeare yield their secrets. But working upon a stage which reproduced the essential conditions of his, working as students, not as showmen merely, a company of actors might well find many of the riddles of the library answering themselves unasked. And these Prefaces could best be a record of such work, if such work were to be done.

We cannot, on the other hand, begin our research by postulating the principles of the Elizabethan stage. One is tempted to say it had none, was too much a child of nature to bother about such things. Principles were doubtless imposed upon it when it reached respectability, and heads would be bowed to the yoke. Shakespeare's among them? He had served a most practical apprenticeship to his trade. If he did not hold horses at the door, he sat behind the curtains, we may be sure, and held the prompt book on occasion. He acted, he cobbled other men's plays, he could write his own to order. Such a one may stay a journeyman if he is not a genius, but he will not become a doctrinaire. Shakespeare's work shows such principles as the growth of a tree shows. It is not haphazard merely because it is not formal; it is shaped by inner strength. The theatre, as he found it, allowed him and encouraged him to great freedom of development. Because the material resources of a stage are simple, it does not follow that the technique of its playwriting will stay so. Crude work may show up more crudely, when there are none of the fal-lals of illusion to disguise it that the modern theatre provides. But, if he has it in him, a dramatist can, so unfettered, develop the essentials of his art more boldly and more subtly too. The Elizabethan drama made an amazingly quick advance from crudity to an excellence which was often technically most elaborate. The advance and the not less amazing gulf which divides its best from its worst may be ascribed to the simplicity of the machinery it employed. That its decadence was precipitated by the influence of the Masque and the shifting of its centre of interest from the barer public stage to the candle-lit private theatre, where the machinery of the Masque became effective, it would be rash to assert; but the occurrences are suspiciously related. Man and machine (here at any rate is a postulate, if a platitude!) are false allies in the theatre, secretly at odds; and when man gets the worst of it, drama is impoverished; and the struggle, we may add, is perennial. No great drama depends upon pageantry. All great drama tends to concentrate upon character; and, even so, not upon picturing men as they show themselves to the world like figures on a stage—though that is how it must ostensibly show them—but on the hidden man. And the progress of Shakespeare's art from *Love's Labour's Lost* to *Hamlet*, and thereafter with a difference, lies in the simplifying of this paradox and the solving of the problem it presents; and the process involves the developing of a very subtle sort of stagecraft indeed.

For one result we have what we may call a very self-contained drama. Its chief values, as we know, have not changed with the fashions of the theatre. It relies much on the music of the spoken word, and a company of schoolchildren with pleasant voices, and an ear for rhythm, may vociferate through a play to some effect. It is as much to be enjoyed in the reading, if we hear it in imagination as we read, as drama meant to be acted can be. As with its simplicities then, so it should be, we presume, with its complexities. The subtly emotional use of verse and the interplay of motive and character, can these not be appreciated apart from the bare boards of their original setting? It does not follow. It neither follows that the advantages of the Elizabethan stage were wholly negative nor that, with our present knowledge, we can imagine the full effect of a play in action upon it. The imagining of a play in action is, under no circumstances, an easy thing.[3] What would one not give to go backward through the centuries to see the first performance of *Hamlet*, played as Shakespeare had it played![4] In default, if we could but make ourselves read it as if it were a manuscript fresh from its author's hands! There is much to be said for turning one's back on the editors, even, when possible, upon the First Folio with its demarcation of acts and scenes, in favour of the Quartos—Dr Pollard's 'good' Quartos—in their yet greater simplicity.

The Convention of Place

It is, for instance, hard to discount the impression made merely by reading: *Scene i—Elsinore. A platform before the Castle*; and most of us have, to boot, early memories of painted battlements and tenth-century castles (of ageing Hamlets and their portly mothers for that matter) very difficult to dismiss. No great harm, one protests; it was a help, perhaps, to the unimaginative. But it is a first step to the certain misunderstanding of Shakespeare's stagecraft. The 'if, how and when' of the presenting of localities on the Elizabethan stage is, of course, a complex question. Shakespeare himself seems to have followed, consciously, no principles in the matter, nor was his practice very logical, nor at all consistent. It may vary with the play he is writing and the particular stage he is writing for; it will best be studied in relation to each play. We can, however, free ourselves from one general misconception which belongs to our own over-logical standpoint. When we learn with a shock of surprise—having begun in the schoolroom upon the Shakespeare of the editors, it comes as belated news to us—that neither battlements, throne rooms nor picturesque churchyards were to be seen at the Globe, and that *Elsinore. A platform before the Castle* is not Shakespeare at all, we yet imagine ourselves among the audience there busily conjuring these things up before the eye of faith. The Elizabethan audience was at no such pains. Nor was this their alternative to seeing the actors undisguisedly concerned with the doors, curtains and balconies which, by the play's requirements, should have been anything but what they were. As we, when a play has no hold on us, may fall to thinking about the scenery, so to a Globe audience, unmoved, the stage might be an obvious bare stage. But are we conscious of the scenery behind the actor when the play really moves us? If we are, there is something very wrong with the scenery, which should know its place as a background. The audience was not conscious of curtain and balcony when Burbage played Hamlet to them. They were conscious of Hamlet. That conventional background faded as does our painted illusion, and they certainly did not deliberately conjure up in its place mental pictures of Elsinore. The genus audience is passive, if expectant, imaginatively lazy till roused, never, one may be sure, at pains to make any effort that is generally unnecessary to enjoyment.

With Shakespeare the locality of a scene has dramatic importance, or it has none; and this is as true of his early plays as his late ones. Both in *Richard II* and *Antony and Cleopatra*, scene after scene passes with no exact indication of where we may be. With *Cleopatra* we are surely in Egypt, with Cæsar in Rome. Pompey appears, and the talk tells us that both Egypt and Rome are elsewhere; but positively where Pompey is at the moment we never learn.[5] Indoors or outdoors? The action of the scene or the clothing of the characters will tell us this if we need to know. But, suddenly transported to the Parthian war, our whereabouts is made amply plain. It is, however, made plain by allusion. The information peeps out through talk of kindred things; we are hardly aware we are being told, and, again, we learn no more than we need to learn. This, truly, is a striking development from the plump and plain

> Barkloughly Castle call they this at hand?

of Richard II, even from the more descriptive

> I am a stranger here in Gloucestershire:
> These high wild hills and rough, uneven ways
> Draw out our miles. . .

by which Shakespeare pictures and localizes the manoeuvres of Richard and Bolingbroke when he wants to.
But the purpose is the same, and the method essentially
the same.[6] Towards the end of the later play come scene
after scene of the marching and countermarching of
armies, of fighting, of truce, all the happenings of three
days' battle. Acts III and IV contain twenty-eight scenes
long and short; some of them are very short; three of
them have but four lines apiece. The editors conscien-
tiously ticket them *A plain near Actium, Another part of the
plain, Another part of the plain* and so on, and conclude that
Shakespeare is really going too far and too fast, is indeed
(I quote Sir Edmund Chambers) 'in some danger of
outrunning the apprehensions of his auditory.' Indeed he
might be if this cinematographic view of his intentions
were the right one! But it utterly falsifies them. Show an
audience such a succession of painted scenes—if you
could at the pace required—and they would give attention to nothing else whatever; the drama would pass
unnoticed. Had Shakespeare tried to define the whereabouts of every scene in any but the baldest phrases—the
protesting editors seem not to see that he makes no
attempt to; only *they* do!—he would have had to lengthen
and complicate them; had he written only a labelling
line or two he would still have distracted his audience
from the essential drama. Ignoring whereabouts, letting
it at most transpire when it naturally will, the characters
capture all attention. This is the true gain of the bare
stage; unless to some dramatic end no precious words
need be spent, in complying with the undramatic demands of space and time; incarnation of character can
be all in all. Given such a crisis as this the gain is yet
greater. We are carried through the phases of the three
days' battle; and what other stage convention would
allow us so varied a view of it, could so isolate the true

drama of it? For do we not pass through such a crisis
in reality with just that indifference to time and place?
These scenes, in their kind, show Shakespeare's stagecraft, not at its most reckless, but at its very best, and
exemplify perfectly the freedom he enjoyed that the stage
of visual illusion has inevitably lost. His drama is at-
tached solely to its actors and their acting; that, perhaps,
puts it in a phrase. They carry place and time with them
as they move. The modern theatre still accepts the
convention that measures time more or less by a play's
convenience; a half-hour stands for an hour or more,
and we never question the vagary. It was no more
strange to an Elizabethan audience to see a street in
Rome turned, in the use made of it, to the Senate House
by the drawing of a curtain and the disclosure of
Cæsar's state, to find Cleopatra's Monument now on the
upper stage because Antony had to be drawn up to it,
later on the lower because Cleopatra's death-scene could
best be played there; it would seem that they were not
too astonished even when Juliet, having taken leave of
Romeo on the balcony of her bedroom and watched him
descend to the lower stage, the scene continuing, came
down, a few lines later, to the lower stage herself,
bringing, so to speak, her bedroom with her—since this
apparently is what she must have done.[7] For neither
Senate House, Monument nor balcony had rights and
reality of their own. They existed for the convenience
of the actors, whose touch gave them life, a shadowy life
at most; neglected, they existed no longer.[8]

Shakespeare's stagecraft concentrates, and inevitably,
upon opportunity for the actor. We think now of the
plays themselves; their first public knew them by their
acting; and the development of the actor's art from the
agilities and funniments of the clown, and from round-
mouthed rhetoric to imaginative interpreting of character

by such standards as Hamlet set up for his players, was
a factor in the drama's triumph that we now too often
ignore. Shakespeare himself, intent more and more upon
plucking out the heart of the human mystery, stimulated
his actors to a poignancy and intimacy of emotional
expression—still can stimulate them to it—as no other
playwright has quite learned to do.

The Speaking of the Verse

His verse was, of course, his chief means to this emotional expression; and when it comes to staging the plays,
the speaking of verse must be the foundation of all study.
The changes of three hundred years have of themselves
put difficulties in our way here; though there are some
besides—as one imagines—of Shakespeare's own making. Surely his syntax must now and then have puzzled
even his contemporaries. Could they have made much
more than we can of Leontes'

> Affection! thy intention stabs the centre;
> Thou dost make possible things not so held,
> Communicat'st with dreams;—How can this be?
> With what's unreal thou coactive art,
> And fellow'st nothing; then, 'tis very credent
> Thou may'st co-join with something; and thou dost;
> And that beyond commission; and I find it,
> And that to the infection of my brains,
> And hardening of my brows.

The confusion of thought and intricacy of language is
dramatically justified. Shakespeare is picturing a ge-
nuinely jealous man (the sort of man that Othello was
not) in the grip of a mental epilepsy. We parse the passage
and dispute its sense; spoken, as it was meant to be, in
a choking torrent of passion, probably a modicum of

sense slipped through, and its first hearers did not find it a mere rigmarole. But we are apt to miss even that much. Other passages, of early and late writing, may always have had as much sound as sense to them; but now, to the casual hearer, they will convey more sound than sense by far. Nor do puns mean to us what they meant to the Elizabethans, delighting in their language for its own sake. Juliet's tragic fantasia upon 'Aye' and 'I' sounds all but ridiculous, and one sympathizes with an actress hesitating to venture on it. How far, apart from the shifting of accents and the recolouring of vowels, has not the whole habit of English speech changed in these three hundred years? In the theatre it was slowing down, one fancies, throughout the eighteenth century; and in the nineteenth, as far as Shakespeare was concerned, it grew slower and slower, till on occasions one thought—even hoped—that shortly the actor would stop altogether. There may have been more than one cause; imitation of the French Augustans, the effort to make antiquated phrases understood, the increasing size of the theatres themselves would all contribute to it. The result, in any case, is disastrous. Elizabethan drama was built upon vigour and beauty of speech. The groundlings may often have deserved Shakespeare's strictures, but they would stand in discomfort for an hour or so to be stirred by the sound of verse. Some of the actors no doubt were robustious periwigpated fellows, but, equally, it was no empty ideal of acting he put into Hamlet's mouth—and Burbage's. We may suppose that at its best the mere speaking of the plays was a very brilliant thing, compared to *bel canto*, or to a pianist's virtuosity. The emotional appeal of our modern music was in it, and it could be tested by ears trained to the rich and delicate fretwork of the music of that day. Most Hamlets—not being playwrights—make a mild joke of telling us they'd as lief the town-crier spoke their lines, but we may hear in it the echo of some of Shakespeare's sorest trials.

The speaking of his verse must be studied, of course, in relation to the verse's own development. The actor must not attack its supple complexities in *Antony and Cleopatra* and *Cymbeline*, the mysterious dynamics of *Macbeth*, the nobilities of *Othello*, its final pastoral simplicities in *A Winter's Tale* and *The Tempest* without preliminary training in the lyricism, the swift brilliance and the masculine clarity of the earlier plays. A modern actor, alas, thinks it simple enough to make his way, splay-footed, through

> The cloud-capped towers, the gorgeous palaces ...

though Berowne's

> I, forsooth, in love ...

or one of Oberon's apostrophes will defeat him utterly. And, without an ear trained to the delicacy of the earlier work, his hearers, for their part, will never know how shamefully he is betraying the superb ease of the later. If we are to make Shakespeare our own again we must all be put to a little trouble about it. We must recapture as far as may be his lost meanings; and the sense of a phrase we *can* recapture, though instinctive emotional response to it may be a loss forever. The tunes that he writes to, the whole great art of his music-making, we can master. Actors can train their ears and tongues and can train our ears to it. We talk of lost arts. No art is ever lost while the means to it survive. Our faculties rust by disuse and by misuse are coarsened, but they quickly recover delight in a beautiful thing. Here, at any rate, is the touchstone by which all interpreting of Shakespeare the playwright must first—and last—be tried.

The Boy-Actress

MORE than one of the conditions of his theatre made this medium of accomplished speech of such worth to him. Boys played the women parts; and what could a boy bring to Juliet, Rosalind or Cleopatra beyond grace of manner and charm of speech? We have been used to women on the stage for two hundred and fifty years or more, and a boy Juliet—if the name on the programme revealed one, for nothing else might—would seem an odd fish to us; no one would risk a squeaking Cleopatra; though, as for Rosalind, through three-parts of the play a boy would have the best of it. But the parts were written for boys; not, therefore, without consideration of how boys could act them most convincingly. Hence, of course, the popularity of the heroine so disguised. The disguise was perfect; the make-believe one degree more complex, certainly, than it needs to be with us; but once you start make-believe it matters little how far you go with it; there is, indeed, some enjoyment in the make-believe itself. But, further, it is Shakespeare's constant care to demand nothing of a boy-actress that might turn to unseemliness or ridicule. He had not much taste for what is called 'domestic drama,' nor does he dose us very heavily with Doll Tearsheet, Mistress Overdone and their like. Constance mourns Arthur's loss, Lady Macduff has her little son, but no mother croons over the child in her arms. Paulina brings Hermione's baby to Leontes, it is true; but see with what tact, from this point of view, the episode is managed. And love-scenes are most carefully contrived. Romeo and Juliet are seldom alone together; never for long, but in the balcony-scene; and in this, the most famous of love-scenes, they are kept from all contact with each other. Consider *Antony and*

Cleopatra. Here is a tragedy of sex without one single scene of sexual appeal. That aspect of Cleopatra is reflected for us in talk about her; mainly by Enobarbus, who is not mealymouthed; but his famed description of her voluptuousness is given us when she has been out of our sight for several scenes. The play opens with her parting from Antony, and in their two short encounters we see her swaying him by wit, malice and with the moods of her mind. Not till the story takes its tragic plunge and sex is drowned in deeper passion are they ever intimately together; till he is brought to her dying there has been occasion for but one embrace. Contrast this with a possible Cleopatra planned to the advantage of the actress of today.

Shakespeare, artist that he was, turned this limitation to account, made loss into a gain.[9] Feminine charm—of which the modern stage makes such capital—was a medium denied him. So his men and women encounter upon a plane where their relation is made rarer and intenser by poetry, or enfranchised in a humour which surpasses more primitive love-making. And thus, perhaps, he was helped to discover that the true stuff of tragedy and of the liveliest comedy lies beyond sensual bounds. His studies of women seem often to be begun from some spiritual paces beyond the point at which a modern dramatist leaves off. Curious that not a little of the praise lavished upon the beauty and truth of them— mainly by women—may be due to their having been written to be played by boys!

Much could be said for the restoring of the celibate stage; but the argument, one fears, would be academic. Here, though, is practical counsel. Let the usurping actress remember that her sex is a liability, not an asset. The dramatist of today may refuse to exploit its allure- ments, but may legitimately allow for the sympathetic effect of it; though the less he does so, perhaps, the better for his play and the more gratitude the better sort of actress will show him. But Shakespeare makes no such demands, has left no blank spaces for her to fill with her charm. He asks instead for self-forgetful clarity of perception, and for a sensitive, spirited, athletic beauty of speech and conduct, which will leave prettiness and its lures at a loss, and the crudities of more Circean appeal looking very crude indeed.

The Soliloquy

THIS convention of the boy-actress may be said to give a certain remoteness to a play's acting. The soliloquy brings a compensating intimacy, and its use was an important part of Shakespeare's stagecraft. Its recognized usefulness was for the disclosing of the plot, but he soon improved upon this. Soliloquy becomes the means by which he brings us not only to a knowledge of the more secret thoughts of his characters, but into the closest emotional touch with them too. Here the platform stage helped him, as the stage of scenic illusion now defeats his purpose. But it is not altogether a question of 'realism' and the supposed obligation this lays upon a real man in a real-looking room to do nothing he would not do if the whole affair were real.

There is no escape from convention in the theatre, and all conventions can be made acceptable, though they cannot all be used indiscriminately, for they are founded in the physical conditions of the stage of their origin and are often interdependent one with another. Together they form a code, and they are as a treaty made with the audience. No article of it is to be abrogated unless we can be persuaded to consent, and upon its basis we surrender our imaginations to the playwright.

With the soliloquy upon the platform stage it is a case—as so often where convention is concerned—of extremes meeting. There is no illusion, so there is every illusion. Nothing very strange about this man, not even the dress he wears, leaning forward a little we could touch him; we are as intimate and familiar with him as it is possible to be. We agree to call him 'Hamlet', to suppose that he is where he says he is, we admit that he thinks aloud and in blank verse too. It is possible that the more we are asked to imagine the easier we find it to do. It is certain that, once our imagination is working, visual illusion will count for little in the stimulating of emotion beside this intimacy that allows the magnetism of personality full play.

There is no more important task for the producer of Shakespeare than to restore to the soliloquy its rightful place in a play's economy, and in particular to regain for it full emotional effect. We now accept the convention frigidly, the actor manoeuvres with it timidly. Banished behind footlights into that other world of illusion, the solitary self-communing figure rouses our curiosity at best. Yet further adapted to the self-contained methods of modern acting, the soliloquy has quite inevitably become a slack link in the play's action, when it should be a recurring reinforcement to its strength. Shakespeare never pinned so many dramatic fortunes to a merely utilitarian device. Time and again he may be feeling his way through a scene for a grip on his audience, and it is the soliloquy ending it that will give him—and his actor—the stranglehold. When he wishes to quicken the pulse of the action, to screw up its tension in a second or so, the soliloquy serves him well. For a parallel to its full effectiveness on Shakespeare's stage we should really look to the modern music-hall comedian getting on terms with his audience. We may measure the response to Burbage's

O, that this too too solid flesh would melt ...

by recalling—those of us that happily can—Dan Leno
as a washerwoman, confiding domestic troubles to a
theatre full of friends, and taken unhindered to their
hearts. The problem is not really a difficult one. If we
solve the physical side of it by restoring, in essentials,
the relation between actor and audience that the intimacy of the platform stage provided, the rest should soon
solve itself.

Costume

THE problem of costume, when it arises, is a subtler one;
nor probably is it capable of any logical solution. Half
the plays can be quite appropriately dressed in the
costume of Shakespeare's own time. It is a false logic
which suggests that to match their first staging we should
dress them in the costume of ours. For with costume
goes custom and manners—or the lack of them. It may
be both a purge and a tonic to the sluggish-fancied
spectator to be shown a Prince of Denmark in coat and
trousers and a Grave-digger in a bowler hat, for remin-
der that here is a play, not a collection of ritualized
quotations. But physic is for the sick; also, there may be
less drastic cures. When archaeology took hold upon the
nineteenth-century mind it became a matter of moment
to lodge Hamlet in historic surroundings; and withers
were wrung by the anachronisms of ducats and a murder
of Gonzago, French rapiers and the rest. A needlessly
teasing difficulty; why reproduce it in terms of a young
man in a dinner jacket searching for a sword—a thing
not likely to be lying about in his modern mother's sitting
room—with which to kill Polonius, who certainly has
window curtains to hide behind instead of arras? This

gain of intimacy—with a Hamlet we might find sitting opposite at a dinner party—may well be a gain in sympathy. It was originally a great gain, a gift to Shakespeare's audience. But we pay too high a price for it.

What was the actual Elizabethan practice in this matter of costuming is not comprehensively known. We can only say safely that, as with other matters, it was neither constant, consistent, nor, from our present point of view, rational. It was based upon the use of the clothes of the time; but these might be freely and fantastically adapted to suit a particular play or advantage some character in it. Dramatic effect was probably the first consideration and the last. There were such fancy dresses as Oberon or Puck or Caliban might wear; there was always the symbolizing of royalty, and a king would wear a crown whenever he could; there was the utility of knowing Romans from Britons by sight in *Cymbeline*, the martial Roman from the effete Egyptian in *Antony and Cleopatra*, and a Scottish lord when you saw him in *Macbeth*, if we may judge by Malcolm's comment upon Rosse's appearance:

> My countryman; and yet I know him not.

Our difficulty, of course, arises mainly over the historical plays. Not over the English Histories, even so; we can dress Richard III or Henry V by the light of our own superior knowledge of what they wore, and never find it clash violently with anything Shakespeare has put on their backs or in their mouths. But when we come to Julius Cæsar plucking open his doublet, to the conspirators against him with their hats about their ears, and to Cleopatra's

> Cut my lace, Charmian.

not to mention British Imogen in her doublet and hose, we must stop and consider.

The common practice is, in these instances, to ignore the details of Shakespeare's text altogether; to dress Cæsar in his toga, Cleopatra in her habit as she lived, with never a stay-lace about her (though, truly, the costumier, let alone, will tend to get his fashion a few thousand years wrong and turn her out more like the wife of Tutankhamen); and as to Imogen and her sur-roundings, we do our best to compromise with skins and woad. This may be a lesser evil than presenting a Cæsar recalling Sir Walter Raleigh and a Cleopatra who would make us think of Mary Queen of Scots, but it is no solution of the problem. For the actors have to speak these lines, and if action and appearance contradict them, credibility is destroyed. And the constant credi-bility of the actor must be a producer's first care. Nor is this all, nor is it, perhaps, the most important thing to consider. The plays are full of reference, direct and indirect, to Elizabethan custom. They are, further, im-pregnated with what we call 'Renaissance feeling', some more, some less, but all to a degree. Now of this last we have a sense which is likelier to be a better help to their appreciation than any newfangled knowledge of the correct cut of Cleopatra's clothes will be! We know Iago for a Machiavellian figure (so called), and miss none of Shakespeare's intention. But if ever two men breathed the air of a sixteenth-century court, Hamlet and Clau-dius of Denmark do, and to relate them in habit and behaviour to the twilight figures of Saxo Grammaticus is as much a misinterpretation as any mauling of the text can be. They exist essentially doubtless—as do all the major characters of the plays—in their perennial humanity. But never let us forget the means by which this deeper truth of them is made vivid and actual. There have been better intellects than Shakespeare's, and poetry as good as his. He holds his supreme place by his dramatist's necessary power of bringing thought and vague emotion to the terms of action and convincing speech; further, and far more than is often allowed, by his peculiar gift of bringing into contribution the commonplace traffic of life. However wide the spoken word may range, there must be the actor, anchored to the stage. However high, then, with Shakespeare, the thought or emotion may soar, we shall always find the transcendental set in the familiar. He keeps this balance constantly adjusted; and, at his play's greatest moments, when he must make most sure of our response, he will employ the simplest means. The higher arguments of the plays are thus kept always within range, and their rooted humanity blossoms in a fertile upspringing of expressive little things. Neglect or misinterpret these, the inner wealth of Shakespeare will remain, no doubt, and we may mine for it, but we shall have levelled his landscape bare.

Shakespeare's own attitude in this matter of costume and customs was as inconsistent as his practice was casual. He knew what *his* Cæsar or Cleopatra would be wearing and would casually drop in a reference to it. Yet the great Romans themselves were aliens to him. The great idea of Rome fired his imagination. Brutus, Cassius and Antony do not turn typical Elizabethan gentlemen; and to the end of that play he is striving to translate Plutarch. Whenever, on the other hand, even for a moment he has made a character all his own, he cannot but clothe it in lively familiar detail. Cleopatra's are the coquetries of a great lady of his own time, in their phrasing, in the savour. When the heights of the tragedy have to be scaled, manners will not so much matter. But if we make her, at the play's beginning, a pseudo-classic, languishing Oriental, we must do it in spite of Shakespeare, not by his help. What then is the solution of this problem, if the sight of the serpent of old Nile in a farthingale will too dreadfully offend us? We can compromise. Look at Tintoretto's and Paolo Veronese's paintings of 'classic' subjects. We accept them readily enough.

Sometimes, within the boundaries of a play, the centuries seem all at odds. *Cymbeline* need not trouble us, its Roman Britain is pure 'once upon a time'. But in *King Lear*, for instance, Shakespeare is at unwonted pains to throw us back into some heathen past. Yet Edmund is another Iago, Edgar might have been at Wittenberg with Hamlet, and Oswald steps straight from the seventeenth-century London streets. Here, though, the dominant barbarism is the important thing; the setting for Goneril and Regan, Lear's tyranny and madness, and Gloucester's blinding. To a seventeenth-century audience Oswald was so identifiable a figure that it would not matter greatly how he dressed; the modern designer of costume must show him up as best he may. Each play, in fine, if it presents a problem at all, presents its own.

The Integrity of the Text

THE text, one says at first blush, can present no problem at all. The plays should be acted as Shakespeare wrote them—how dispute it? They should be; and it is as well, before we discuss hard cases, to have the principle freely admitted. Lip service enough is done it nowadays, and Colley Cibber's *Richard III*, Tate's *Lear* and Garrick's improvements are at the back of our bookshelves, but we still find Messrs John Doe and Richard Roe slicing out lines by the dozen and even a scene or so, or chopping and changing them to suit their scenery. This will not do. Shakespeare was not a perfect playwright; there can be no such thing. Nor did he aim at a mechanical perfection, but a vitality, and this he achieved. At best then, we cut and carve the body of a play to its peril. It may be robustly, but it may be very delicately organized. And we still know little enough of the laws of its existence, and some of us, perhaps, are not such very skilful surgeons; nor is any surgeon to be recommended who operates for his own convenience.

This good rule laid down, what are the exceptions that go to prove it? There is the pornographic difficulty. This is not such a stumbling block to us as it was to Bowdler, to some bright young eyes nowadays it is quite imperceptible, in fact. Yet, saving their presence, it exists; for it exists aesthetically. Shakespeare's characters often make obscene jokes. The manners of his time permitted it. The public manners of ours still do not. Now the dramatic value of a joke is to be measured by its effect upon an audience, and each is meant to make its own sort of effect. If then, instead of giving them a passing moment's amusement, it makes a thousand people uncomfortable and for the next five minutes very self-conscious, it fails of its true effect. This argument must not be stretched to cover the silliness of turning 'God' into 'Heaven' and of making Othello call Desdemona a 'wanton' (the practice, as I recollect, of the eighteen-nineties), nor to such deodorizing of *Measure for Measure* that it becomes hard to discover what all the fuss is about. If an audience cannot think of Angelo and the Duke, Pompey and Lucio, Isabella and Mistress Overdone, and themselves to boot, as fellow-creatures all, the play is not for them. Othello must call Desdemona a 'whore', and let those that do not like it leave the theatre; what have such queasy minds to do with the pity and terror of her murder and his death? Again, to make Beatrice so mealymouthed that she may not tell us how the devil is to meet her at the gates of hell, 'like an old cuckold with horns on his head', is to dress her in a crinoline, not a farthingale. But suppression of a few of the more scabrous jokes will not leave a play much the poorer; nor, one may add, will the average playgoer be much the wiser or merrier for hearing them, since they are often quite hard to understand.

Topical passages are a similar difficulty. With their savour, if not their very meaning lost, they show like dead wood in the living tree of the dialogue and are better, one would suppose, cut away. But no hard and fast rule will apply. Macbeth's porter's farmer and equivocator will never win spontaneous laughter again. But we cannot away with them, or nothing is left of the porter. Still the baffled low comedian must not, as his wont is, obscure the lines with bibulous antics. There will be that little dead spot in the play, and nothing can be done about it. Rosencrantz' reference to the 'eyrie of children' is meaningless except to the student. Is the play the poorer for the loss of it? But the logic that will take this out had better not rob us of

> Dead shepherd, now I find thy saw of might;
> Who ever loved that loved not at first sight?

And there is the strange case of

The lady of the Strachy married the yeoman of the wardrobe.

Nobody knows what it means, but everybody finds it funny when it is spoken in its place. And this has its parallels.

In general, however, better play the plays as we find them. The blue pencil is a dangerous weapon; and its use grows on a man, for it solves too many little difficulties far too easily.

Lastly, for a golden rule, whether staging or costuming or cutting is in question, and a comprehensive creed, a producer might well pin this on his wall: Gain Shakespeare's effects by Shakespeare's means when you can; for, plainly, this will be the better way. But gain Shakespeare's effects; and it is your business to discern them.

1927

Notes

1 But it should not be forgotten that Sir Herbert Tree, happy in the orthodoxy of public favour, welcomed the heretic Mr Poel more than once to a share in his Shakespeare Festivals.

2 I do not deal in general therefore with certain vexed questions, such as act-division, which still need to be looked at, I think, in the light of the particular play.

3 I remember a most intelligent reader of a modern play missing the whole point of a scene through which the chief character was to sit conspicuously and eloquently silent. He counted only with the written dialogue. I remember, when I thought I knew *King Lear* well enough, being amazed at the effect, all dialogue apart, of the mere meeting, when I saw it, of blind Gloucester and mad Lear.

4 Though, in a sense, there was no first performance of *Hamlet*. And doubtless many of the audience for Shakespeare's new version of the old play only thought he had spoiled a good story of murder and revenge by adding too much talk to it.

5 Unless it may be said that we learn in the scene after whereabouts he *was*.

6 And in *Coriolanus*, which probably postdates *Antony and Cleopatra*, with Marcius' 'A goodly city is this Antium,' we are back to the barely informative. It serves Shakespeare's purpose; he asks no more.

7 I fancy, though, that the later Shakespeare would have thought this a clumsy device.

8 How far this is true of other dramatists than Shakespeare I do not pretend to say; nor how far, with him, the influence of the private theatre, making undoubtedly towards the scenic stage

and (much later) for illusion, did not modify his practice, when he had that stage to consider. A question, again, for the bibliographers and historians.

9   There is no evidence, of course, that he felt it a loss, no such reference to the insufficiency of the boy-actress as there is to the overself-sufficiency of the clown. Women did appear in the Masques, if only to dance, so the gulf to be bridged was not a broad one. But the Elizabethan was as shocked by the notion of women appearing upon the public stage as the Chinese playgoer is today.

Julius Cæsar

JULIUS CÆSAR is the gateway through which Shakespeare passed to the writing of his five great tragedies. He had *Henry V* close behind him, *Hamlet* was not far ahead; between times he writes the three mature comedies, *Much Ado About Nothing, As You Like It* and *Twelfth Night*. In the themes, emphasis and methods of the work of this year or two we may watch the consummating development of his art.

Henry V gives the last touch to a hero of happy destiny. We might call it the latest play in which rhetoric for rhetoric's sake prevails. Shakespeare makes it occasion for a complaint of the inadequacy of his theatre to his theme. And it is, as one says, altogether a man's play. Woman's interest rules the three comedies; further, they contain much prose and make no extraordinary demands upon staging or acting. *Julius Cæsar*, again, is the manliest of plays. For the first time, too, Shakespeare fully submits his imagination to the great idea of Rome; new horizons seem to open to him, and there is to be no return to the comparative parochialism of the Histories. Nor, with this far mightier theme to develop, do we have any hint of discontent with the means to his hand. No Chorus bows apology for the bringing of the foremost man of all the world upon such an unworthy scaffold.[1] And for Philippi, not only must a few ragged foils suffice, we are back to the simple convention by which whole armies face each other across the stage. His playwright's mind is clearly not troubled by such things now. What chiefly occupies it in the planning and writing of *Julius Cæsar*? He is searching, I think we may answer, for a hero, for a new sort of hero. The story offers him more than one, and does not force him to a choice. He chooses, in the event, but haltingly. Very significantly, however.

From the beginning Shakespeare's dramatic development has lain in the discovering and proving of the strange truth that in the theatre, where external show seems everything, the most effective show is the heart of a man. No need to suppose it was lack of resource in stage furnishings drove him to the drama of inward struggle, triumph and defeat. That choice was innermostly made, and no playwright worth calling one but will make it on demand, whatever the theatre he writes for. Henry V is not weakened as a character by lack of a pawing charger, but neither would he be more of a hero set astride one. In himself he is by no means all rhetoric; witness the scene with his father and the soliloquy before Agincourt. But his career has the power and the glory for an end; and the parade of this, at its best, only cumbers your hero—at its worst may make him ridiculous. Henry finishes a fine figure of a man; but long enough before Shakespeare has done all he can with him, and our retrospect is rather of the youthful junketings with Falstaff. For his next hero it is in quite another direction he turns. The next true hero is Hamlet: and Hamlet, foreshadowed in Rosaline's Romeo, in Richard II, in Jaques, is imminent in Brutus. A hero, let us be clear, is the character of which a dramatist, not morally, but artistically, most approves. Macbeth is a hero. Shakespeare's sympathy with Brutus does not imply approval of the murder of Cæsar; it only means that he ultimately finds the spiritual problem of the virtuous murderer the most interesting thing in the story. Brutus best interprets the play's theme: Do evil that good may come, and see what does come!

He is more interested, as he always has been, in character than in plot. He pays, goodness knows, small respect to the plots of the three contemporary comedies; they live by character alone. This, however, is history again, and plot must count. But it is not the homespun of Holinshed, nor the crude stuff of the *Famous Victories*. Plutarch gives him, not only the story he must abide by, but characters already charged with life. His task now is less to elaborate or invent than to capture and transmit as much of such events and such men as his little London theatre will hold. It is a feat of stagecraft to show us so many significant facets of this more than personal tragedy, a finer one to share out the best of the play's action among three chief characters and yet hardly lessen the strength of any of them.

But Shakespeare will never be too sure that he understands these Romans. He does not instinctively know their minds, as he knew Henry's or Hotspur's or Falstaff's. He is even capable of transcribing a fine-sounding passage from Plutarch and making something very like nonsense of it. He never gets to grips with Cæsar himself; whether from shrewd judgment that he could not manoeuvre such greatness in the space he had to spare, or, as looks more likely, from a sort of superstitious respect for it. In which case—well, idols, as we know, are apt to be wooden. Casca, raw from Plutarch, has mettle enough to ride off with a scene or two. Decius Brutus, Ligarius, Lucilius are lifted whole from his pages. And the story itself and its power, once Shakespeare is in its grip, can breed from him moment after moment of pure drama. In no earlier play do the very messengers and servants partake as they do in this. But Brutus, Cassius and Antony, though he has found them alive, he must set out to recreate in his own terms. He does it by trial and error, with a slip here and there, not disdaining a ready-made patch that comes handy; the transformation is never, perhaps, complete. But he seems to be giving them their fling, tempting them to discover themselves, passionate himself to know the truth of them, whatever it may be, and ready to face it. From no other play, probably, does he learn so much in the writing. Collaborating with Plutarch he can be interpreter and creator too. He finds what is to him a new world of men, which he tests for dramatic worth by setting it on this stage of his. *Julius Cæsar* is an occasion to which he rises, his greatest so far; it is a point of advance, from which he never falls back.

The Characters

BRUTUS

THAT the development of Brutus should be slow is proper enough; such characters do not too readily reveal themselves. Shakespeare builds the man up for us trait by trait; economically, each stroke of value, seldom an effect made merely for its own sake. With his usual care that the first things we learn shall be essential things, that very first sentence—measured, dispassionate, tinged with disdain—by which Brutus transmits to Cæsar the cry in the crowd:

A soothsayer bids you beware the Ides of March.

gives us so much of the man in perfection; and its ominous weight is doubled in his mouth, its effect trebled by the innocent irony. Brutus draws aside from the procession to the games, withdrawn into himself.

I am not gamesome: I do lack some part
Of that quick spirit that is in Antony.
Let me not hinder, Cassius, your desires;
I'll leave you.

The strain of self-consciousness, that flaw in moral strength! A suspicion of pose! But self-consciousness can be self-knowledge; Shakespeare holds the scales even.

> Into what dangers would you lead me, Cassius,
> That you would have me seek into myself
> For that which is not in me?

Wisdom itself, could give no apter warning. But is this next passage, in Brutus, something of a flourish, or in Shakespeare a touch of an earlier quality?

> What is it that you would impart to me?
> If it be aught toward the general good,
> Set honour in one eye and death i' the other,
> And I will look on both indifferently;
> For let the gods so speed me as I love
> The name of honour more than I fear death.

It will be captious to call it so. The lines come hard upon the first of those shouts which are perhaps the acclaiming of Cæsar as king. Brutus is not a passionless man, though he may both despise passion and dread it. A minute later he is saying:

> I would not, so with love I might entreat you,
> Be any further mov'd.

Let the actor be wary, however, with that moment of rhetoric; and let him see that his Brutus does not compete here with Cassius. For the jealous, passionate Cassius, to whom and to whose mood eloquence and rhetoric are natural, must indisputably dominate this scene.

Brutus, if we are to learn more of him, needs a different setting. It is soon found. We see him in the calm of night. He is kindly to his sleepy page, gracious to his guests. We see him alone with his wife, left all alone in the quiet with his thoughts. Much comment has been spent upon the first soliloquy in this scene:

> It must be by his death: and, for my part,
> I know no personal cause to spurn at him. . . .

Wise editors have found this inconsistent, some with their own ideal of Brutus, some, rather more reasonably, with the fully drawn figure of Shakespeare's play. But, at this stage of its development, why should we be puzzled? If the argument is supersubtle and unconvincing, why should it not be? It may be that Shakespeare himself is still fumbling to discover how this right-minded man can commit his conscience to murder, and why should his Brutus not be fumbling too? This is how it will seem to an audience, surely.

The scene's marrow is the working of Brutus' mind, alone, in company. He is working it to some purpose now. But because it is, by disposition, a solitary mind, unused to interplay, and because the thoughts are not yet fused with emotion, that commoner currency between man and man, the scene may seem to move a little stiffly and Brutus himself to be stiff. Is not this, again, dramatically right? Would he not speak his thoughts starkly, while the rest only listen and acquiesce?—though Cassius does interpose one broken sentence of protest. They respect him, this upright, calm, self-contained man. He can command, but he cannot stir them; he is not a born leader. If the scene lacks suppleness and ease, one thought not prompting another revealingly, if it burns bright and hard, with never a flash into flame, so it would have been. But see how Shakespeare finally turns this very stiffness and suppression to a greater emotional account, when, after the silence Brutus keeps in the scene with Portia, the cry is wrung from him at last:

> You are my true and honourable wife,
> As dear to me as are the ruddy drops
> That visit my sad heart.

For let no one imagine that the overwhelming effect of this lies in the lines themselves. It has been won by his long impassiveness; by his listening, as we listen to Portia, till he and we too are overwrought. It is won by the courage with which Shakespeare holds his dramatic course.

Our sympathy with Brutus has next to weather the murder, through the planning and doing of which he stalks so nobly and disinterestedly and with such admirable self-control, and our interest in him to survive the emotional storm raised and ridden by Antony. This last might, one would think, sweep him forever from his place in the play. The contriving of his recovery is, indeed, a most remarkable technical achievement. It depends upon several things. For one, upon Shakespeare's honest but ruthless treatment of Antony and his appeal to the mob; we too may be carried away by his eloquence, but the worth of it and of the emotions it rouses is kept clear to us all the time. For another: had he, as playwright, not been faithful to Brutus and his stern consistency, Brutus would fail him now; but now, the emotional debauch over, the stoic's chance is due. And the fourth act opens, it will be remembered, with a most unpleasant glimpse of Antony, the plain blunt man, triumphant, coolly dealing out death sentences—

> These many then shall die; their names are pricked.

—and, as coolly, preparing to leave his colleague Lepidus in the lurch. After that the stage is reset for Brutus and his tragedy.

In the clash with Cassius, Shakespeare, intent upon the truth about the man, shows him, we may protest, no undue favour.

> CASSIUS. Most noble brother, you have done me wrong.
> BRUTUS. Judge me, you gods! wrong I mine enemies?
>   And, if not so, how should I wrong a brother?
> CASSIUS. Brutus, this sober form of yours hides wrongs;
>   And when you do them——
> BRUTUS.   Cassius, be content;
>   Speak your griefs softly. . . .

By the stoic's moral code it is Cassius himself, of course, who is in the wrong. But which of us might not side with him against this comrade, who, with war declared, will be just to his enemies; and, with things going desperately for his side, must needs stiffen his stiff conscience against some petty case of bribery? Is this a time for pride in one's principles? Cæsar is dead—what matter now why or how?—and the spoils must be scrambled for, and the devil will take the hindmost. Cassius is no mere opportunist; yet so weary and distracted is he, that it almost comes to this with him. And he is answered:

> What! shall one of us
> That struck the foremost man of all this world
> But for supporting robbers, shall we now
> Contaminate our fingers with base bribes,
> And sell the mighty space of our large honours
> For so much trash as may be grasped thus?

Noble sentiments doubtless! But to depreciate and dispirit your best friends, to refuse their apologies for having lost patience with you, to refuse even to lose your own in return? Brutus tries many of us as high as he tries Cassius. And what is so quelling to the impulsive, imperfect human being as the cold realism of the idealist?

> CASSIUS. When Cæsar liv'd, he durst not thus have mov'd me.
> BRUTUS. Peace, peace! you durst not so have tempted him.
> CASSIUS. I durst not?
> BRUTUS. No.
> CASSIUS. What? durst not tempt him?
> BRUTUS.   For your life you durst not.

Supercilious, unforgiving—and in the right! And when anger does rise in him, it is such a cold, deadly anger that poor passionate Cassius only breaks himself against it. Yet there is a compelling power in the man, in his integrity of mind, his truth to himself, in his perfect simplicity. Even the detached, impersonal,

> CASSIUS. You love me not.
> BRUTUS.   I do not like your faults.
> CASSIUS. A friendly eye could never see such faults.
> BRUTUS. A flatterer's would not. . . .

though we may palate it no better than its immediate hearer does, is and sounds the simple truth. Cassius cannot, somehow, be simple. The dagger and the naked breast—who would be more surprised than he, we feel, were he taken at his word? But when Brutus relents his moral guard goes down so utterly; there sweeps over him such a sense of the pitifulness, not of Cassius and his self-conscious passion only, but of all these petty quarrels of human nature itself, of his own:

> When I spoke that I was ill-tempered too.

It is a child making friends again with his fellow-child.

Shakespeare has now all but prepared us for the scene's great stroke; for the winning stroke in Brutus' own cause with us. The quarrel is over and the 'jigging fool' has been dismissed. Cassius took his turn as mentor when Brutus snapped at the wretched poet.

> Bear with him, Brutus, 'tis his fashion.[2]

They set themselves to their business and call for a bowl of wine; we are in the vein of workaday. The one confesses to his 'many griefs'; the other responds with kindly platitude. And to this comes the simple answer, three naked words completing it:

BRUTUS. No man bears sorrow better: Portia is dead.
CASSIUS. Ha! Portia!
BRUTUS. She is dead.
CASSIUS. How 'scaped I killing when I crossed you so!

The seal is set upon Brutus' pre-eminence in the play, which from now to its end is to be, in its main current, the story of the doom towards which he goes unregretful and clear-eyed.

Hamlet, we have said, originating in Richard and Romeo, is imminent in Brutus; but the line of descent is broken. Shakespeare, we may add, fails in Brutus just where he will succeed in Hamlet; he is instinctively searching, perhaps, to express something which the poet in Hamlet will accommodate, which the philosopher in Brutus does not. Having lifted his heroic Roman to this height, he leaves him, we must own, to stand rather stockishly upon it. There is more than one difficulty in the matter; and they were bound to come to a head. Brutus reasons his way through life, and prides himself upon suppressing his emotions. But the Elizabethan conventions of drama—and most others—are better suited to the interpreting of emotion than thought. The soliloquy, certainly, can be made a vehicle for any sort of intimate disclosure. Shakespeare has converted it already from a direct telling of the story or a length of sheer

rhetoric, but not to turn it into a length of mere reasoning. His actors could, indeed, better hope to hold their
audiences by fine sounds than by mental process alone.
Brutus' soliloquies in Act II are all but pure thought,
and in their place in the play, and at this stage of his
development, are well enough, are very well. But—does
Shakespeare feel?—you cannot conduct a tragedy to its
crisis so frigidly. Had Brutus been the play's true and
sole hero a way might have been found (by circling him,
for instance, with episodes of passion) to sustain the
emotional tension in very opposition to his stoic calm.
The murder of Cæsar and its sequel sweeps the play up
to a passionate height. The quarrel with the passionate
Cassius, and the fine device of the withheld news of
Portia's death, lift Brutus to an heroic height without
any betrayal of the consistent nature of the man. But
now we are at a standstill. Now, when we expect nemesis
approaching, some deeper revelation, some glimpse of
the hero's very soul, this hero stays inarticulate, or,
worse, turns oracular. The picturing of him is kept to
the end at a high pitch of simple beauty; but when—so
we feel—the final and intimate tragic issue should open
out, somehow it will not open. When Cæsar's ghost
appears:

BRUTUS. Speak to me what thou art.
GHOST. Thy evil spirit, Brutus.
BRUTUS.   Why com'st thou?
GHOST. To tell thee thou shalt see me at Philippi.
BRUTUS. Well: then I shall see thee again.
GHOST. Ay, at Philippi.
BRUTUS. Why, I will see thee at Philippi, then.

That may be true Brutus, but it comes short of what we
demand from the tragic hero of this calibre. And before
Philippi, a step nearer to the end of this work the Ides

of March began, we have from the philosopher so
confused a reflection on his fate that we may well
wonder whether Shakespeare himself, transcribing it
from a mistranslated Plutarch, is quite certain what it
means.[3]

We are left with

> O! that a man might know
> The end of this day's business ere it come;
> But it sufficeth that the day will end,
> And then the end is known.

That is the voice, they are all but the very words of
Hamlet. Shakespeare is to run the gamut of the mood
of helpless doubt—the mood which has kept Hamlet our
close kin through three disintegrating centuries—to more
if not to better purpose. With Brutus it but masks the
avoiding of the spiritual issue. And he is sent to his
death, a figure of gracious dignity, the noblest Roman
of them all, but with eyes averted from the issue still.

> Countrymen,
> My heart doth joy that yet in all my life
> I found no man but he was true to me. . . .
> Night hangs upon mine eyes; my bones would rest,
> That have but labour'd to attain this hour.

The plain fact is, one fears, that Shakespeare, even if
he can say he understands Brutus, can in this last
analysis *make* nothing of him; and no phrase better fits
a playwright's particular sort of failure. He has let him
go his own reasoning way, has faithfully abetted him in
it, has hoped that from beneath this crust of thought the
fires will finally blaze. He can conjure up a flare or two,
and the love and grief for Portia might promise a fusing
of the man's whole nature in a tragic passion outpassing
anything yet. But the essential tragedy centred in Brutus'

own soul, the tragedy of the man who, not from hate, envy nor weakness, but

> only, in a general honest thought
> And common good to all . . .

made one with the conspirators and murdered his friend; this, which Shakespeare rightly saw as the supremely interesting issue, comes to no more revelation than is in the last weary

> Cæsar, now be still:
> I killed not thee with half so good a will.

Shakespeare's own artistic disposition is not sufficiently attuned to this tragedy of intellectual integrity, of principles too firmly held. He can appreciate the nature of the man, but not, in the end, assimilate it imaginatively to his own. He is searching for the hero in whom thought and emotion will combine and contend on more equal terms; and when the end of Brutus baffles him, here is Hamlet, so to speak, waiting to begin. For the rest, he at least reaps the reward, better than Brutus did, of integrity and consistency. He never falsifies the character, and, in its limited achievement, it endures and sustains the play to the end. He had preserved, we may say, for use at need, his actor's gift of making effective things he did not fully understand; and the Brutus of the play will make call enough upon any actor, even should he know a little more about the historic Brutus—whom, after all, he is not here called on to understand—than Shakespeare did.

CASSIUS

Cassius, the man of passion, is set in strong contrast to Brutus, the philosopher; and to stress the first impression he himself will make on us, we have Cæsar's own grimly humorous assessment of him:

> Yond Cassius has a lean and hungry look;
> He thinks too much: such men are dangerous. . . .
> I fear him not;
> Yet if my name were liable to fear,
> I do not know the man I should avoid
> So soon as that spare Cassius. He reads much;
> He is a great observer, and he looks
> Quite through the deeds of men; he loves no plays,
> As thou dost, Antony; he hears no music;
> Seldom he smiles, and smiles in such a sort
> As if he mocked himself, and scorned his spirit
> That could be moved to smile at any thing.
> Such men as he be never at heart's ease
> Whiles they behold a greater than themselves,
> And therefore are they very dangerous. . . .

—a Puritan, that is to say, something of an ascetic, and with the makings of a fanatic in him too. Already it will not be, to Shakespeare's audience, a wholly unfamiliar figure. A dangerous man, doubtless; and as much so sometimes to his friends, they will feel, as to his enemies.

> Into what dangers would you lead me, Cassius,
> That you would have me seek into myself
> For that which is not in me?

the besought Brutus protests. At the best a man difficult to deal with; jealous and thin-skinned; demanding much of his friends, and quick to resent even a fancied slight. His very first approach to Brutus:

> I do observe you now of late:
> I have not from your eyes that gentleness
> And show of love as I was wont to have. . . .

And in their later quarrel the burden of his grievance is

You love me not.

An egoist certainly; yet not ignobly so, seeking only his own advantage. Convinced in a cause—as we find him convinced; that Cæsar's rule in Rome must be free Rome's perdition—he will fling himself into it and make no further question, argue its incidental rights and wrongs no more, as Brutus may to weariness. For argument will have now become a kind of treason. There lie doubt and the divided mind, which he detests in others, and would dread in himself, since there lies weakness too, while passion will carry him through, and give him power to goad others on besides. Egoist he is, yet not intellectually arrogant. He sees in Brutus the nobler nature and a finer mind, and yields to his judgment even when he strongly feels that it is leading them astray. These principles! It would have been practical good sense to add Antony's death to Cæsar's; it was foolish to a degree—rapidly it proved so—to let him speak in the market place later; that was a petty business, after all, about Lucius Pella and his bribes; and to what does Brutus' insistence on his strategy lead them but to Philippi? It is as if he felt that in some such yielding fashion he must atone for those outbursts of rage that he will not control. And yet, despite exasperating failings, the man is lovable, as those which are spendthrift of themselves can be, and as—for all his virtues—Brutus is not.

Cassius is by no means all of a piece, and makes the more lifelike a character for that. He ruthlessly demands Antony's death (the cause demands it), but in a desperate crisis, with danger threatening, he can take sudden thought for Publius' age and weakness. He has marked respect for Brutus; but he does not scruple to play tricks on him, with the letter laid in the Prætor's chair, the

placard pinned to the statue. And, despite his outbursts of
passion, he can calculate at times pretty coolly. Why does
he not go with the rest on that fatal morning to conduct
Cæsar to the Senate House? He has said he will go—

> Nay, we will all of us be there to fetch him.

—and it will not be sudden timidity, certainly, that sways
him. Do second thoughts suggest that since Cæsar, as he
knows, mistrusts him, his presence may rouse suspicion?
Shakespeare leaves this to be implied—or not, since we
may not remark his absence. Yet he has been so promi-
nent a figure in the earlier scenes, that we can hardly
help remarking it.[4]

He is cynical, and can be brutally downright. While
Brutus is appealing to Antony's higher nature (Cæsar
dead there between them) he comes out plump with a

> Your voice shall be as strong as any man's
> In the disposing of new dignities.

But his deep affection for Brutus rings true; even in the
midst of their quarrel, when he hears of Portia's death,
as they mutually say farewell.

> BRUTUS. For ever, and for ever, farewell, Cassius!
>   If we do meet again, why, we shall smile;
>   If not, why then this parting was well made.
> CASSIUS. For ever, and for ever, farewell, Brutus!
>   If we do meet again, we'll smile indeed;
>   If not, 'tis true this parting was well made.

—there is harmony in the echoing exchange itself; and
they do not meet again.

The cynical Cassius shows in the soliloquy:

> Well, Brutus, thou art noble; yet, I see,
> Thy honourable metal may be wrought

> From that it is disposed: therefore 'tis meet
> That noble minds keep ever with their likes;
> For who so firm that cannot be seduced? . . .

—it is at this very moment that he is scheming to seduce
his much-admired friend by the papers thrown in at his
window and other such devices. Beneath his enthusiasms
and rash humours there is a certain coldness of passion,
which gives him tenacity, lets him consider and plan, the
tension of his temper never slackening; and it is in this
combination of opposites that the man is most dangerous. He will put his very faults to use, do things for his
cause that he never would for himself, yet not, as with
Brutus, studiously justifying them. His hatred for Cæsar
the tyrant may well be rooted in jealousy of Cæsar the
man; if so, he is at no pains to disguise it. But he is
incapable of protesting his love for him at one moment,
while—on principle—he will strike him down the next.

So forthcoming a man, so self-revealing as he naturally
is, what character could better animate the play's opening, and get the action under way? But there must soon
come a check. No play can continue at such a strain, to
the fatiguing of actors and audience both. It comes with
this very soliloquy,

> Well, Brutus, thou art noble. . . .

and here, if Shakespeare meant to dig deeper into
Cassius' nature, would be the chance. But he avoids it.
Brutus is to be the introspective character, the play's
spiritual hero, so to speak; and there will not be room
for two. Nor (as we said) is Cassius the man to spend
time in self-searching, though he urges Brutus to. So the
soliloquy—the only one allotted him—matched against
the extraordinary vitality of the earlier dialogue, falls a
little flat, runs somewhat mechanically, rather too closely

resembles one of those conventional plot-forwarding dis-
courses to the audience, to which Shakespeare has long
learned to give richer use; and it demands the final
whip-up of that rhymed couplet. At this juncture, then,
and for a while longer we learn little more about Cassius.
In the scene of the storm that follows he is eloquent and
passionate still. But it is the same gamut that he runs.
And in the scenes which follow this he strikes the same
notes, of a rather arid desperation. Not until the later
quarrel with Brutus is he fully and strikingly reanimated;
but then indeed the intimacy opens up, of which we
shall have felt deprived before. We have no deliberate
and explanatory self-confession (that, again, belongs to
Brutus), simply an illustrative picture of Cassius in word
and action, companion to that earlier one.

He has not changed, yet circumstances have changed
him. In that paradox lies the tragedy of such natures.
He was jealous of Cæsar then, and he has turned jealous
of Brutus now; of his friend as he was of his enemy. So
Cæsar read him aright:

> Such men as he be never at heart's ease
> Whiles they behold a greater than themselves. . . .

He slights Brutus' generalship as he once contemned
Cæsar's courage. He is as quick and as shrewd and as
shrewish as ever. But then it was:

> Well, honour is the subject of my story. . . .

and now he is prudently excusing a rogue, with his own
honour in question. The one-time eloquent candour has
turned to blustering and scolding. Yet, even while he
rages, he knows he is in the wrong. His pride is little
more than a mask. And the lofty Brutus has but to soften
towards him—one touch of simple humanity suffices—
and he breaks down like a child. He is pleading now:

> O, Brutus!
>> What's the matter?
> Have you not love enough to bear with me,
> When that rash humour which my mother gave me
> Makes me forgetful?

And from now on, as if—so we noted—in atonement, he will follow the younger man's mistaken lead, convinced as he is that it is mistaken. He only craves affection:

>> O, my dear brother,
> This was an ill beginning of the night:
> Never come such division 'tween our souls!
> Let it not, Brutus.

abases himself—he, the elder soldier—with that

> Good night, my lord.

the now indulgent Brutus quickly preventing him with a

> Good night, good brother.

But thus it is with these catastrophic natures. They spend themselves freely, but demand half the world in exchange. They behave intolerably, try their friends' patience beyond all bounds, confidently expecting, for the sake of their love for them, to be forgiven. They know and confess to their faults, but with no intention of amendment; you must take them, they say, 'as they are'.

> Old Cassius still!

mocks Antony, when the two meet again, parleying before the battle. And certainly the sharp tongue is by then as sharp as ever. At which point we remark too that the quarrel with Brutus and the reconciliation after have proved to Cassius both relief and comfort. For despite ill-omens, and his unchanged distrust in Brutus' soldiership, he proclaims himself

> fresh of spirit and resolved
> To meet all perils very constantly.

But, the battle joined, in the fury of fancied defeat he will kill his own standard-bearer, and himself, in his impatient despair. Old Cassius still!

ANTONY

> There is a tide in the affairs of men,
> Which, taken at the flood, leads on to fortune. . . .

Mark Antony cannot always talk so wisely, but he takes the tide that Brutus loses. He is a born opportunist, and we see him best in the light of his great opportunity. He stands contrasted with both Cassius and Brutus, with the man whom his fellows respect the more for his aloofness, and with such a rasping colleague as Cassius must be. Antony is, above all things, a good sort.

Shakespeare keeps him in ambush throughout the first part of the play. Up to the time when he faces the triumphant conspirators he speaks just thirty-three words. But there have already been no less than seven separate references to him, all significant. And this careful preparation culminates as significantly in the pregnant message he sends by his servant from the house to which it seems he has fled, bewildered by the catastrophe of Cæsar's death. Yet, as we listen, it is not the message of a very bewildered man. Antony, so far, is certainly—in what we might fancy would be his own lingo—a dark horse. And, though we may father him on Plutarch, to English eyes there can be no more typically English figure than the sportsman turned statesman, but a sportsman still. Such men range up and down our history. Antony is something besides, however, that we used to flatter ourselves was not quite so English. He can be, when occasion serves, the perfect demagogue. Nor has Shakespeare any illusions as to what the harsher needs of politics may convert your sportsman once he is out to kill. The conspirators are fair game doubtless. But Lepidus, a little later, will be the carted stag.

> A barren-spirited fellow; one that feeds
> On abject orts and imitations,
> Which, out of use and staled by other men,
> Begin his fashion: do not talk of him
> But as a property . . .

to serve the jovial Antony's turn! This is your good sort, your sportsman, your popular orator, stripped very bare.

The servant's entrance with Antony's message, checking the conspirators' triumph, significant in its insignificance, is the turning point of the play.[5] But Shakespeare plucks further advantage from it. It allows him to bring Antony out of ambush completely effective and in double guise; the message foreshadows him as politician, a minute later we see him grieving deeply for his friend's death. There is, of course, nothing incompatible in the two aspects of the man, but the double impression is all-important. He must impress us as uncalculatingly abandoned to his feelings, risking his very life to vent them. For a part of his strength lies in impulse; he can abandon himself to his feelings, as Brutus the philosopher cannot. Moreover, this bold simplicity is his safe-conduct now. Were the conspirators not impressed by it, did it not seem to obliterate his politic side, they might well and wisely take him at his word and finish with him then and there. And at the back of his mind Antony has this registered clearly enough. It must be with something

of the sportsman's—and the artist's—happy recklessness
that he flings the temptation at them:

> Live a thousand years,
> I shall not find myself so apt to die:
> No place will please me so, no mean of death,
> As here by Cæsar, and by you cut off,
> The choice and master spirits of this age.

He means it; but he knows, as he says it, that there is
no better way of turning the sword of a so flattered
choice and master spirit aside. It is this politic, shadowed
aspect of Antony that is to be their undoing; so Shakespeare is concerned to keep it clear at the back of our
minds too. Therefore he impresses it on us first by the
servant's speech, and Antony himself is free a little later
to win us and the conspirators both.

Not that the politician does not begin to peep pretty
soon. He tactfully ignores the cynicism of Cassius,

> Your voice shall be as strong as any man's
> In the disposing of new dignities.

But by Brutus' reiterated protest that Cæsar was killed
in wise kindness what realist, what ironist—and Antony
is both—would not be tempted?

> I doubt not of your wisdom.
> Let each man render me his bloody hand. . . .

And, in bitter irony, he caps their ritual with his own.
It is the ritual of friendship, but of such a friendship as
the blood of Cæsar, murdered by his friends, may best
cement. To Brutus the place of honour in the compact;
to each red-handed devotee his due; and last, but by no
means least, in Antony's love shall be Trebonius who
drew him away while the deed was done. And so to the
final, most fitting apostrophe:

Gentlemen all!

Emotion subsided, the politician plays a good game.
They shall never be able to say he approved their deed;
but he is waiting, please, for those convincing reasons
that Cæsar was dangerous. He even lets slip a friendly
warning to Cassius that the prospect is not quite clear.
Then, with yet more disarming frankness, comes the
challenging request to Brutus to let him speak in the
market place. As he makes it, a well-calculated request!
For how can Brutus refuse, how admit a doubt that the
Roman people will not approve this hard service done
them? Still, that there may be no doubt at all, Brutus
will first explain everything to his fellow-citizens himself,
lucidly and calmly. When reason has made sure of her
sway, the emotional, the 'gamesome', Antony may do
homage to his friend.

> Be it so;
> I do desire no more.

responds Antony, all docility and humility, all gravity—
though if ever a smile could sharpen words, it could give
a grim edge to these. So they leave him with dead Cæsar.

In this contest thus opened between the man of high
argument and the instinctive politician, between principle (mistaken or not) and opportunism, we must remember that Antony can be by no means confident of
success. He foresees chaos. He knows, if these bemused
patriots do not, that it takes more than correct republican
doctrines to replace a great man. But as to this Roman
mob—this citizenry, save the mark!—whoever knows
which way it will turn? The odds are on the whole against
him. Still he'll try his luck; Octavius, though, had better
keep safely out of the way meanwhile. All his senses are
sharpened by emergency. Before ever Octavius' servant

can speak he has recognized the fellow and guessed the errand. Shakespeare shows us his mind at its swift work, its purposes shaping.

> Passion, I see, is catching, for mine eyes,
> Seeing those beads of sorrow stand in thine,
> Began to water.

—from which it follows that if the sight of Cæsar's body can so move the man and the man's tears so move him, why, his own passion may move his hearers in the market place presently to some purpose! His imagination, once it takes fire, flashes its way along, not by reason's slow process though in reason's terms.[6]

To what he is to move his hearers we know: and it will be worth while later to analyze the famous speech, that triumph of histrionics.[7] For though the actor of Antony must move us with it also—and he can scarcely fail to—Shakespeare has set him the further, harder and far more important task of showing us an Antony the mob never see, of making him clear to us, moreover, even while we are stirred by his eloquence, of making clear to us just by what it is we are stirred. It would, after all, be pretty poor playwriting and acting which could achieve no more than a plain piece of mob oratory, however gorgeous; a pretty poor compliment to an audience to ask of it no subtler response than the mob's. But to show us, and never for a moment to let slip from our sight, the complete and complex Antony, impulsive and calculating, warm-hearted and callous, aristocrat, sportsman and demagogue, that will be for the actor an achievement indeed; and the playwright has given him all the material for it.

Shakespeare himself knows, no one better, what mere histrionics may amount to. He has been accused of showing in a later play (but unjustly, I hold) his too great

contempt for the mob; he might then have felt something
deeper than contempt for the man who could move the
mob by such means; he may even have thought Brutus
made the better speech. Antony, to be sure, is more than
an actor; for one thing he writes his own part as he goes
along. But he gathers the ideas for it as he goes too,
with no greater care for their worth than the actor need
have so long as they are effective at the moment. He
lives abundantly in the present, his response to its call
is unerring. He risks the future. How does the great
oration end?

> Mischief, thou are afoot;
> Take thou what course thou wilt!

A wicked child, one would say, that has whipped up his
fellow-children to a riot of folly and violence. That is
one side of him. But the moment after he is off, brisk,
cool and businesslike, to play the next move in the game
with that very cool customer, Octavius.

He has had no tiresome principles to consult or to
expound.

> I only speak right on. . . .

he boasts;

> I tell you that which you yourselves do know. . . .

An admirable maxim for popular orators and popular
writers too! There is nothing aloof, nothing superior
about Antony. He may show a savage contempt for this
man or that; he has a sort of liking for men in the mass.
He is, in fact, the common man made perfect in his
commonness; yet he is perceptive of himself as of his
fellows, and, even so, content.

What follows upon his eloquent mourning for Cæsar?
When the chaos in Rome has subsided he ropes his

'merry fortune' into harness. It is not a very pleasant colloquy with which the fourth act opens.

> ANTONY. These many then shall die; their names are pricked.
> OCTAVIUS. Your brother too must die; consent you, Lepidus?
> LEPIDUS. I do consent.
> OCTAVIUS. Prick him down, Antony.
> LEPIDUS. Upon condition Publius shall not live,
> Who is your sister's son, Mark Antony.
> ANTONY. He shall not live; look, with a spot I damn him.

The conspirators have, of course, little right to complain. But four lines later we learn that Lepidus himself, when his two friends have had their use of him, is to fare not much better than his brother—than the brother he has himself just given so callously to death! Can he complain either, then? This is the sort of beneficence the benevolent Brutus has let loose on the world.

But Antony finishes the play in fine form; victorious in battle, politicly magnanimous to a prisoner or two, and ready with a resounding tribute to Brutus, now that he lies dead. Not in quite such fine form, though: for the shadow of that most unsportsmanlike young man Octavius is already moving visibly to his eclipse.

These, then are the three men among whom Shakespeare divides this dramatic realm; the idealist, the egoist, the opportunist. The contrast between them must be kept clear in the acting by all that the actors do and are, for upon its tension the living structure of the play depends. And, it goes without saying, they must be shown to us as fellow-creatures, not as abstractions from a dead past. For so Shakespeare saw them; and, if he missed something of the mind of the Roman, yet these three stand with sufficient truth for the sum of the human forces, which in any age, and in ours as in his, hold the world in dispute.

OCTAVIUS CÆSAR

He tags to the three another figure; and perhaps nothing in the play is better done, within its limits, than is the outline of Octavius Cæsar, the man who in patience will reap when all this bitter seed has been sown. He appears three times, speaks some thirty lines, and not one of them is wasted. We see him first with Antony and Lepidus. He watches them trade away the lives of their friends and kinsmen. And when Antony, left alone with him, proposes to 'double-cross' Lepidus, he only answers,

> You may do your will;
> But he's a tried and valiant soldier.

It is the opening of a window into this young man's well-ordered mind. Lepidus is a good soldier, he approves of Lepidus. But Antony is powerful for the moment, it won't do to oppose Antony. Lepidus must suffer then. Still, should things turn out differently, let Antony remember that this was his own proposal, and that Octavius never approved of it.[8]

By the next scene, however, this quiet youth has grown surer—not of himself, that he has no need to be, but of his place amid the shifting of events.

ANTONY. Octavius, lead your battle softly on,
  Upon the left hand of the even field.
OCTAVIUS. Upon the right hand, I; keep thou the left.
ANTONY. Why do you cross me in this exigent?
OCTAVIUS. I do not cross you; but I will do so.

He is quite civil about it; but he means to have his way, his chosen place in the battle and chief credit for the victory. And Antony does not argue the point. When the opponents in the coming battle are face to face, Cassius and Antony and even Brutus may outscold each the other for past offences. The practical Octavius, with a mind to the present and to his own future, is impatient of such childishness.

> Come, come, the cause: if arguing make us sweat,
> The proof of it will turn to redder drops.
> Look, I draw sword against conspirators;
> When think you that the sword goes up again?
> Never, till Cæsar's three-and-thirty wounds
> Be well aveng'd; or till another Cæsar
> Have added slaughter to the sword of traitors.

This is the first time he has spoken out, and he speaks to some purpose. Nor does he give place to Antony again. When we see them together for the last time in victorious procession, Octavius has the lead.

> All that serv'd Brutus, I will entertain them.

'I', not 'we'. And Shakespeare gives him the play's last word.

CÆSAR

What now of the great shadow of Cæsar which looms over the whole? Let us admit that, even while he lives and speaks, it is more shadow than substance. Is it too harsh a comment that Cæsar is in the play merely to be assassinated? But to have done better by him would have meant, would it not, doing worse by the play as it is planned? Certainly to centre every effort—and it could hardly be done with less—upon presenting to us the foremost man of all this world . . .

and then to remove him at the beginning of Act III
would leave a gap which no new interest could fill. But
there are innate difficulties in the putting of any great
historical figure upon the stage: and these, as it happens,
would have pressed hard upon Shakespeare just at this
stage of his development. He had left behind him the
writing of that formal rhetoric which was the accepted
dramatic full dress for the great man. He was moulding
his verse to the expressing of individual emotion, fitting
his whole method to the showing of intimate human
conflict. Now a great man's greatness seldom exists in
his personal relations. To depict it, then, the dramatist
will be thrown back on description, or narrative, or on
the effect of the greatness upon the characters around.
The last expedient may shift our interest to the surround-
ing characters themselves. Narrative soon becomes tiresome. And as to description; the great man himself, in
the person of his actor, is too apt to belie it. Keep him
immobile and taciturn, and the play will halt. But if he
talks of his own achievements he will seem a boaster.
And if he is always seen in action we can have no picture
of the inner man. The convention of Greek drama offers
some escape from these dilemmas; for there the man is,
so to speak, made in his greatness a symbol of himself,
and in a symbol one may sum up a truth. Shakespeare
had, certainly, the refuge of soliloquy. Show us the heart
of a Cæsar, though, by that means, and where will our
interest in the self-revealings of a Brutus be? And it is,
we have argued, upon Brutus' spiritual tragedy that
Shakespeare's best thoughts are fixed. He comes, therefore, to showing us a Cæsar seen somewhat from Brutus'
point of view; a noble figure and eloquent, but our
knowledge of him stays skin-deep. It is historically

possible, of course, that the virtue had gone out of Cæsar, that no more was left now than this façade of a great man. But we need not credit Shakespeare with the theory. Quite certainly he wishes to show us the accepted Cæsar of history. The innate difficulty of doing so may defeat him; the limitations of the play, as he has planned it, must. And if he has to choose, and it becomes a question of his play's safety, Cæsar will count no more with him than any other character.

But it follows that, as he cannot attempt to do Cæsar dramatic justice, the more we see of him the worse it is. For the devices by which his supremacy can be made effective are soon exhausted and do not bear repetition. The start is excellent. What could be more impressive than that first procession across the stage? Here Shakespeare tries the taciturn-immobile method, and couples it with a strict simplicity of speech; all one can call a trick is the repetition of the name, and Cæsar's own use of it, and even this is legitimate enough. While, for a finish, the confronting of the Soothsayer:

> CASSIUS. Fellow, come from the throng; look upon Cæsar.
> CÆSAR. What say'st thou to me now? Speak once again.
> SOOTHSAYER. Beware the Ides of March.
> CÆSAR. He is a dreamer; let us leave him: pass.

Here is the great man; assuming no attitude, explaining nothing, indifferent to seeming trifles. What could be better? The last line is pure gold.

The episode of the returning procession is as good. That sidelong perceptive survey of Cassius with its deep-biting humour:

> Let me have men about me that are fat,
> Sleek-headed men, and such as sleep a-nights.
> Yond Cassius has a lean and hungry look;
> He thinks too much: such men are dangerous.

The yet deeper-bitten realism of

> He reads much;
> He is a great observer, and he looks
> Quite through the deeds of men; he loves no plays,
> As thou dost, Antony; he hears no music;
> Seldom he smiles, and smiles in such a sort
> As if he mock'd himself, and scorn'd his spirit
> That could be mov'd to smile at any thing.
> Such men as he be never at heart's ease
> Whiles they behold a greater than themselves,
> And therefore are they very dangerous.

The precise simplicity of thought and language mark the man raised above his fellows. Do we need, then,

> I rather tell thee what is to be fear'd
> Than what I fear, for always I am Cæsar.

But it is from this very moment that the direct picturing of Cæsar turns to talk about Cæsar by Cæsar. Fine talk; but the living man is lost in it. For a line or two he may emerge, only to be lost again in some such operatic sonority as

> Cæsar should be a beast without a heart
> If he should stay at home to-day for fear.
> No, Cæsar shall not; danger knows full well
> That Cæsar is more dangerous than he:
> We are two lions littered in one day,
> And I the elder and more terrible;
> And Cæsar shall go forth.

—while the Olympian speech in the Senate House leaves one a little surprised that a moment later blood can be supposed to flow from him. Shakespeare, in fact, has now slipped not merely into this queer *oratio obliqua* but back to the discarded rhetoric for its own sake, though the writing of the characters round Cæsar stays directly dramatic enough. The actor must effect what sort of reconciliation he can between this simulacrum of greatness and the dramatic life around. To think of Cæsar as now no more than an empty shell, reverberating hollowly, the life and virtue gone out of him, is one way. It must weaken the play a little; for will it be so desperate an enterprise to conspire against such a Cæsar? Or is such a frigid tyranny the more dangerous of the two? But the supersubtlety of that interpretation is worse.

CASCA AND THE REST

Among the men no other characters reach primary importance. Casca is effective rather than important, and the only question about him is of the break from prose to verse (as between Act I, Scenes ii and iii), which points a kindred but hardly warrantable break in the composition of the character itself. It is all very well to say with Dowden that Casca appears in the storm with his 'superficial garb of cynicism dropt', and that, while dramatic consistency may be a virtue, Shakespeare here gives us an instance of 'a piece of higher art, the dramatic inconsistency of his characters'. If it were so the thing would still be very clumsily done. What means is the actor given of showing that this is a dramatic inconsistency? We never see one flutter of that superficial garb of cynicism again. Casca remains hereafter the commonplace Casca of the storm-scene; the humorous blunt fellow seems forgotten quite. Certainly we have had Cassius' apology for him, that he

puts on this tardy form . . .

But the passage in which that occurs is itself weak and mechanical, and it might arguably have been written in to excuse the clumsiness of the change. The actor must do what he can to weld the two halves of the man together; but it is doubtful whether he can make this 'piece of higher art' very valid.

The producer must remember that nine-tenths of the play is, so to speak, orchestrated for men only; the greater the need in the casting of the parts to set them in due contrast with each other. The sort of acting a part needs is usually made plain enough; if not by some reference, acting itself will test this. For instance, if nothing definitely directs us to make the Flavius and Marullus of the first scene a mild man and a masterfully noisy one, yet in the acting they will be found to answer effectively to that difference. For the casting of Cicero, on the other hand, we have definite, if mainly *ex post facto*, direction; his elderly dry irony is set, when the two meet, in strong contrast with the new ebullient Casca. It is to be noted, by the way, that Shakespeare, history apart, thinks of the conspirators as fairly young men. By theatrical tradition Caius Ligarius is made old as well as ill, but there is nothing to warrant this (for an ague does not warrant it), nor any dramatic gain in it.

Cinna the poet is specified plainly enough in the dandification of

> What is my name? Whither am I going? Where do I dwell? Am I a married man or a bachelor? Then, to answer every man directly and briefly, wisely and truly; wisely I say, I am a bachelor.

The nameless poet of Act IV must be even more eccentric if his flying visit is to be made effective. Cassius calls him a cynic. He is, one supposes, a shabby, balladmongering fellow; his modern instance shuffles through the *cafés* of Montmartre today. Shakespeare, rapt in this world of great doings, is a little hard on poets—as some poets are apt to be.

The soldiers that belong to the play's last phase, Messala, Lucilius, Titinius, young Cato, Pindarus, Volumnius, Strato and the rest, can all be known for what they are by considering what they do. In no play, I think, does Shakespeare provide, in such a necessarily small space, for such a vivid array. As parts of a battle-piece, the unity of the subject harmonizes them, but within that harmony each is very definitely and effectively himself.

CALPURNIA AND PORTIA

The boy Lucius has sometimes been played by a woman. This is an abomination. Let us not forget, on the other hand, that Calpurnia was written to be played by a boy. Producers are inclined to make a fine figure of her, to give her (there being but two women in the play) weight and importance, to fix on some well-proportioned lady, who will wear the purple with an air. But Shakespeare's intention is as plain as daylight; and in a part of twenty-six lines there can be no compromise, it must be hit or miss. Calpurnia is a nervous, fear-haunted creature. Nor does she, like Portia, make any attempt to conceal her fears. She is desperate and help-less. Portia, with her watchful constancy, can win Brutus' secret from him. Cæsar treats Calpurnia like a child. Her pleading with him is a frightened child's pleading. Her silence when Decius and the rest come to fetch him to the Senate House is as pathetic in its helplessness. She stands isolated and tremulous, watching him go in to taste some wine with these good friends. Failing the right sort of Calpurnia, the dramatic value of her share in the scene will be lost.

A quiet beauty is the note of Portia, and Shakespeare sounds it at once. Her appearance is admirably contrived. The conspirators have gone, Brutus is alone again, and the night's deep stillness is recalled.

> Boy! Lucius! Fast asleep? It is no matter;
> Enjoy the honey-heavy dew of slumber:
> Thou hast no figures nor no fantasies
> Which busy care draws in the brains of men;
> Therefore thou sleep'st so sound.

But so softly she comes, that for all the stillness he is unaware of her, until the soft voice, barely breaking it, says,

> Brutus, my lord!

Portia is a portrait in miniature. But how suited the character itself is to such treatment, and how Shakespeare subdues his power to its delicacy! The whole play is remarkable for simplicity and directness of speech; nothing could exemplify her better. For she is seen not as a clever woman, nor is she witty, and she speaks without coquetry of her 'once-commended beauty'. She is homekeeping and content; she is yielding, but from good sense, which she does not fear will seem weakness. She has dignity and perfect courage.

Note how everything in the scene—not the words and their meaning only—contributes to build up this Portia. The quiet entrance, the collected thought and sustained rhythm of her unchecked speech, the homely talk of supper-time and of the impatient Brutus scratching his head and stamping, and of the risk he is running now of catching cold; nothing more wonderful than this is the foundation for the appeal to

> that great vow
> Which did incorporate and make us one . . .

Nor does the appeal at its very height disturb the even music of the verse. For with her such feelings do not ebb and flow; they lie deep down, they are a faith. She is, as we should say, all of a piece; and her very gentleness, her very reasonableness is her strength. Even her pride has its modesty.

> I grant I am a woman, but, withal,
> A woman that Lord Brutus took to wife;
> I grant I am a woman; but, withal,
> A woman well-reputed, Cato's daughter;
> Think you I am no stronger than my sex,
> Being so father'd and so husbanded?

The repeated phrase and the stressed consonants give the verse a sudden vigour; they contrast with the drop back to simplicity of

> Tell me your counsels, I will not disclose 'em.
> I have made strong proof of my constancy,
> Giving myself a voluntary wound
> Here, in the thigh: can I bear that with patience
> And not my husband's secrets?

To this, with imperceptibly accumulating force, with that one flash of pride for warning, the whole scene has led. A single stroke, powerful in its reticence, as fine in itself as it is true to Portia.

Then, lest she should seem too good to be true, Shakespeare adds a scene of anticlimax; of a Portia confessing to weakness, all nerves, miserably conscious that her page's sharp young eyes are fixed on her; outfacing, though, the old Soothsayer, and, with a final effort, spiritedly herself again. While, for one more touch of truth, he gives us,

> O Brutus!
> The heavens speed thee in thine enterprise.

Murder is the enterprise, and Cato's daughter knows it.
But he is her Brutus, so may the heavens speed him
even in this.

The Play's Structure

THERE is a powerful ease in the construction of *Julius
Cæsar* which shows us a Shakespeare master of his means,
and it is the play in which the boundaries of his art
begin so markedly to widen. We find in it, therefore, a
stagecraft, not of a too accustomed perfection, but bold
and free. The theme calls forth all his resources and
inspires their fresh and vigorous use; yet it does not strain
them, as some later and, if greater, less accommodating
themes are to do. We may here study Elizabethan
stagecraft, as such, almost if not quite at its best; and a
close analysis of the play's action, the effects in it and
the way they are gained—a task for the producer in any
case—will have this further interest.

Plutarch was a godsend to Shakespeare. Rome, Cæsar
and high heroic verse, one knows what such a mixture
may amount to in the theatre; though we may suppose
that, with his lively mind, he would never have touched
the subject had he not found that admirable historian,
who, with happy familiarity, tucks an arm in ours, so to
speak, and leads us his observant, anecdotic way, huma-
nizing history, yet never diminishing its magnificence.
Plutarch's genius, in fact, is closely allied to Shakespeare's own, with its power to make, by a touch or so
of nature, great men and simple, present and past, the
real and the mimic world, one kin. And this particular
power was in the ascendant with Shakespeare now.

He redraws the outline of the story more simply, but
he cannot resist crowding characters in. What wonder,
when they are all so striking, and he knows he can make

a living man out of a dozen lines of dialogue? The fifth act is a galaxy of such creations. And if, on the other hand, Artemidorus and the Soothsayer have little or no life of their own, while the poet of Act IV is a mere irruption into the play, a species of human ordnance shot off, their momentarily important part in the action lends them reflected life enough. But much of the play's virtue lies in the continual invention and abundant vitality of these incidental figures by which the rarer life, so to call it, of the chief characters is at intervals nourished. And as there is no formal mechanism of plot, it is largely with their aid that the action moves forward with such a varied rhythm, upon an ebb and flow of minor event that is most lifelike. The whole play is alive; it is alive in every line.

Elizabethan stagecraft, with its time-freedom and space-freedom, gives the playwright great scope for manoeuvring minor character and incident. He may conjure a character into sudden prominence, and be done with it as suddenly. He has not, as in the modern 'realistic' theatre, to relate it to the likelihoods of hard-and-fast time and place. The modern dramatist plans his play by large divisions, even as the Greek dramatist did. Time and place must suit the need of his chief characters; if minor ones can't be accommodating they can't be accommodated, that's all. The Elizabethan dramatist has his story to tell, and the fate of the chief figures in it to determine. But, as long as the march of the story is not stayed, he may do pretty well what he likes by the way. The modern dramatist thinks of his play constructively in acts; and the scenes must accommodate themselves to the act, as the acts to the play as a whole. The Elizabethan would instinctively do the contrary. This is not to say that a play did not commonly move to some larger rhythm than the incidental. Every playwright, every sort of artist indeed, feels for the form which will best accommodate his idea, and will come to prefer the comprehensive form. But whether this rhythm with Shakespeare resolved itself into acts is another matter; and that it would resolve itself into the five acts of the editors is more than doubtful.

The larger rhythm of *Julius Cæsar* can be variously interpreted. The action moves by one impetus, in a barely checked crescendo, to the end of Act III. Cæsar's murder is the theme; the mob provides a recurrent chorus of confusion, and ends, as it has begun, this part of the story. Acts IV and V are given to the murder's retribution; this unifies them. They are martial, more ordered, and, for all the fighting at the end, consistently pitched in a lower key. The five-act division can, however, be defended dramatically; and, if it is valid, it shows us some interesting points of Elizabethan stagecraft. Act I is preparatory and leads up to the conspirators' winning of Brutus, though this itself is kept for the start of Act II. Modern practice would dictate a division after Act I, Sc. ii; for here is a time interval and a change from day to night. But to Shakespeare—or his editor—it would be more important to begin a new act upon a new note, and with the dominant figure of Brutus to impress us. And this we find: each act of the five has a significant and striking beginning, while the ends of the first four all tail away. Act III begins with the ominous

> CÆSAR.   The Ides of March are come.
> SOOTHSAYER. Ay, Cæsar, but not gone.

Act IV with the sinister

> ANTONY. These many then shall die; their names are pricked.

Act V with the triumphant

OCTAVIUS. Now, Antony, our hopes are answered. . . .

It is easy to see why the beginning of an Elizabethan 'act' had to be striking.[9] There was no lowering of the lights, no music, no warning raps, while eyes 'in front' concentrated upon an enigmatic curtain. The actors had to walk on and command the unprepared attention of a probably restless audience, and they needed appropriate material. Equally, to whatever crisis of emotion a scene might mount, they would have to walk off again. Therefore neither acts nor scenes, as a rule, end upon a crisis.

The play is too strenuous, if not too long, to be acted without at least one pause. It must occur, of course, at the end of Act III. This one should, I personally think, be enough; if pauses are to mean long intervals of talk and distraction, it certainly would be. But if a producer thinks more relief from the strain upon the audience is advisable (his actors do not need it), there is the breathing-space at the end of Act II—better not make more of it—and, if that will not suffice, he can pause at the end of Act I. He will be unwise, though, to divide Acts IV and V.

But the form of the play should first be studied in relation to its minor rhythms, for it is in these, in the setting of them one against the other, in their adjustment to the larger rhythm of the main theme, that the liveliness of Shakespeare's stagecraft is to be seen.

The action begins with the entry of the two Tribunes . . . *and certain commoners over the stage.* The Roman populace is to play an important part; we have now but a minute's glimpse of it, and in harmless holiday mood.

> Hence! home, you idle creatures, get you home:
> Is this a holiday?

The first lines spoken are a stage direction for the temper of the scene. It may be that the Globe Theatre 'crowd' was not much of a crowd, was liable to be unrehearsed and inexact. Line after line scattered through the scene is contrived to describe indirectly how they should look and what they should be expressing. No audience but will accept the suggestion, though the crowd itself be a bit behindhand. Nor need a producer, here or elsewhere, strive to provide a realistically howling mob. The fugleman convention is a part of the convention of the play; reason enough for abiding in it.

Note before we leave this scene how its first full-bodied speech has Pompey for a theme, and what emphasis is given to the first sound of his name. After the chattering prose of the cobbler comes Marullus'

> Wherefore rejoice? What conquest brings he home?
> What tributaries follow him to Rome
> To grace in captive bonds his chariot wheels?
> You blocks, you stones, you worse than senseless things!
> O you hard hearts, you cruel men of Rome,
> Knew you not Pompey?

For Pompey dead is to Cæsar something of what Cæsar dead is to be to Brutus and the rest. And—though Shakespeare naturally does not prejudice an important effect by anticipating it and elaborating its parallel—the name's reiteration throughout the first part of the play has purpose.

A unity is given to these first three acts by the populace; by keeping them constantly in our minds. They are easily persuaded now, controlled and brought to silence:

> They vanish tongue-tied in their guiltiness.

The devastation of the third act's end has this mild beginning.

Against the disorder and inconsequence, Cæsar's processional entrance tells with doubled effect. We are given

but a short sight of him, our impression is that he barely
pauses on his way. His dominance is affirmed by the
simplest means. We hear the name sounded—sounded
rather than spoken—seven times in twenty-four lines.
The very name is to dominate. It is the cue for Cassius'
later outburst:

> Brutus and Cæsar: what should be in that 'Cæsar'?
> Why should that name be sounded more than yours?
> Write them together, yours is as fair a name;
> Sound them, it doth become the mouth as well;
> Weigh them, it is as heavy; conjure with 'em,
> 'Brutus' will start a spirit as soon as 'Cæsar'.

The procession passes. And now that these opposites, the
many-headed and the one, the mob and its moment's
idol, have been set in clear contrast before us, the main
action may begin.

It is Cassius' passion that chiefly gives tone and colour
to the ensuing long duologue. He sets it a swift pace too,
which is only checked by Brutus' slow responses; Brutus,
lending one ear to his vehement friend, the other keen
for the meaning of the distant shouts. Yet, in a sense, it
is Cæsar who still holds the stage; in Cassius' rhetoric,
in the shouting, in Brutus' strained attention. With his
re-entrance, then, there need be no impression given of
a fresh beginning, for the tension created by that first
passage across the stage should hardly have been relaxed. It now increases, that is all. Cæsar pauses a little
longer on his way, and with purpose. It is like the passing
of a thundercloud; presage, in another sort, of the storm
by which Nature is to mark his end. To the stately words
and trumpet music the procession moves on; and we are
left, with the proper shock of contrast, to Casca's acrid
and irreverent prose. Now the tension does relax. Then
Casca goes, and Brutus and Cassius part with but brief

comment on him, without attempting to restore the broken harmony of their thoughts; and Cassius' closing soliloquy, as we have seen, is little more than a perfunctory forwarding of the story.

Thunder and lightning...

This, the stage empty, would emphasize well enough for the Elizabethans some break of time and place, and a few claps and flashes more might suffice to put a whole storm on record. It does not now suffice Shakespeare. He sets out upon a hundred and sixty-five lines of elaborate verbal scene-painting; in the economy of the plot they really stand for little more. It is not, of course, merely a passing pictorial effect that he is branding on his audience's imagination. Consider this passage in connection with those appeals of the Chorus in *Henry V*:

> Think when we talk of horses that you see them
> Printing their proud hoofs i' the receiving earth;
> For 'tis your thoughts that now must deck our kings...

>   O! do but think
> You stand upon the rivage and behold
> A city on the inconstant billows dancing;
> For so appears this fleet majestical,
> Holding due course to Harfleur.

All that the listeners were to do for themselves, since the dramatist could not even attempt to do it for them. Here Shakespeare is certainly concerned to picture Rome under the portentous storm, but it is upon the personal episodes he fixes—upon the slave with his burning hand, the

>   hundred ghastly women,
> Transformed with their fear, who swore they saw
> Men all in fire walk up and down the streets...

upon the marvel of the lion that 'glar'd upon' Casca and 'went surly by'. And their value to him lies chiefly in their effect upon the emotions of his characters; this is his path to an effect upon ours. He has discovered, in fact, the one dramatic use to which the picturesque can be put in his theatre, and the one and only way of using it. It was not, of course, a discovery sought and made all complete for the occasion. But this is, I think, the first time he brings Nature under such serious contribution. Make another comparison, with the storm-scenes in *King Lear*. Set this scene beside those, with their perfect fusion of character and surroundings and their use to the play, and its method seems arbitrary and crude enough. It takes the plot little further. And Cicero is a walking shadow, Cinna a mere convenience; Casca, unnerved and eloquent, is unrecognizable as the Casca of the previous scene, is turned to a convenience for picturing the storm; while Cassius only repeats himself, and his rhetoric, dramatically justified before, grows rodomontade. By the end of the hundred and sixty-five lines we have learned that Cicero is cautious, Casca ripe, that things are moving fast with Cinna and the rest, that Brutus must be won. At his best Shakespeare could have achieved this in fifty lines or less and given us the storm into the bargain.

The contrasting calm of the next act's beginning is an appropriate setting for Brutus, the stoic, the man of conscience and gentle mind. The play's scheme now opens out and grows clear, for Brutus takes his allotted and fatal place among his fellows as moral dictator. To his dominance is due the scene's coldness and rigidity, though the unity of tone gives it dignity and its circumstance alone would make effective drama. Incidental things give it vitality and such colour as it needs; the coming and going of the sleepy boy, the knocking without, the striking of the clock followed by those three short echoing speeches. It all stays to the end rather static than dynamic; for high-mindedly as Brutus may harangue his 'gentle friends', fervently as they may admire him, there is never, now or later, the spontaneous sympathy between them that alone gives life to a cause. The ultimate as well as the immediate tragedy is in the making.

The scene with Portia is the due sequel. Even from her he holds aloof. He loves her; but the more he loves her the less he can confide in her. Even the avowal of his love is wrung from him in a sort of agony. And Portia's own tragedy is in the making here. In her spent patience with his silence we might well divine the impatience at his absence which was to be her death. We may question why, after a vibrant climax, Shakespeare so lowers the tension for the scene's end. Caius Ligarius' coming will surely thrust Portia and this more intimate Brutus to the background of our remembrance. There are two answers at least. The play's main action must not only be carried on, but it must seem now to be hurried on, and Brutus, his philosophic reserve once broken, must be shown precipitate.[10] For another answer; the Caius Ligarius episode keeps the scenes between Brutus and Portia, Cæsar and Calpurnia apart. It would discount the second to bring it on the heels of the first.

Thunder and lightning herald the next scene's beginning; the purpose of its repetition is plain enough. The mood wrought in us by the storm must be restored; and in a moment comes Calpurnia's speech, which is a very echo of Casca's description of the signs and portents. Cæsar, rocklike at first against the pleadings of his wife, wavers from his love for her and yields to Decius' friendliness and flattery, reinforced by the thronging-in of the rest, looking, as Brutus bid them look, so 'fresh and merrily'. It is good preparation for the catastrophe, the sudden livening of the scene with this group of resolute, cheerful men. Besides, might not the slim Decius have overreached himself but for their coming? Cæsar was no fool, and Calpurnia would be apt to every sort of suspicion. But the friendly faces disperse the last clouds of the ominous night. Cassius is not here. It is Brutus, the irreproachable Brutus, who gives tone to the proceeding. Does he, even at this moment, feel himself

> arm'd so strong in honesty . . .

that he can meet Cæsar's magnanimity without flinching? Is it only ague that makes Caius Ligarius shake as Cæsar presses his hand? And that nothing of tragic irony may be wanting—

> Good friends, go in, and taste some wine with me,
> And we, like friends, will straightway go together.

The sacrament of hospitality and trust! It is a supreme effect, economized in words, fully effective only in action. And for an instance of Shakespeare's dramatic judgment, of his sense of balance between an immediate effect and the play's continuing purpose, of his power, in striking one note, to strike the ruthlessly right one, take the two lines with which Brutus, lagging back, ends the scene:

> That every like is not the same, O Cæsar!
> The heart of Brutus yearns to think upon.

Not that a pun or a quibble upon words necessarily struck an Elizabethan as a trifling thing. But it takes a Brutus to find refuge in a quibbling thought at such a moment, and in his own grief for his victim.

Cæsar is now ringed by the conspirators, the daggers are ready, and the two scenes that follow are to hold and prolong the suspense till they strike." Artemidorus, with his paper and its comment, may seem unduly dry and detached. But the solitary anonymous figure comes as a relief and contrast to that significant group, and against that wrought emotion his very detachment tells. It contrasts too with Portia's tremulous intimate concern. The act's end here—if it is to mean a short empty pause while the audience stay seated and expectant, not an interval of talk and movement—will have value. The blow is about to fall, and in silence suspense is greatest. We draw breath for the two long scenes that form the centre section of the play.

Trumpets sound, the stage fills. Cæsar comes again as we saw him go, still circled by these friends, confident, outwardly serene. The trumpets silent, we hear another prelude, of two voices, the one ringing clear, the other pallidly echoing:

CÆSAR.   The Ides of March are come.
SOOTHSAYER. Ay, Cæsar, but not gone.

Then follows a little scuffle of voices, a quick shifting and elbowing in the group round Cæsar as the petitions are thrust forward and aside, and once again that five-fold iteration of the potent name. Despite the ceremony, nerves are on edge. Cæsar goes forward to be greeted by the Senators and to mount his state. Now comes a passage of eighteen lines. Toneless it has to be, that the speakers betray not their feelings. In the group of them there is hardly a movement; they must measure even their glances. Popilius Lena's threading his way through them is startling in itself. Yet on this monotone the whole gamut of the conspiracy's doubts, fears and desperation is run. Its midway sentence is the steely

Cassius, be constant. . . .

with which Brutus marks his mastery of the rest. Cæsar is seated. His turns the whole concourse to him. Some few of them are ready indeed. And now, in terms of deliberate rhetoric, Shakespeare once more erects before us the Colossus that is to be overthrown. Then in a flash the blow falls. Butchered by Casca, sacrificed by Brutus— these two doings of the same deed are marked and kept apart—Cæsar lies dead.

Remark that we are now only a quarter of the way through the scene; further, that the play's whole action so far has been a preparation for this crisis. Yet, with dead Cæsar lying there, Shakespeare will contrive to give us such fresh interest in the living that, with no belittling of the catastrophe, no damping-down nor desecration of our emotions, our minds will be turned forward still. This is a great technical achievement. He might well have shirked the full attempt and have wound up the scene with its next seventy lines or so. But then could the play ever have recovered strength and impetus? As it is, by the long scene's end our concern for Cæsar is lost in our expectations of the Forum. The producer must note carefully how this is brought about, lest even the minor means to it miscarry.

The mainspring of the renewed action will lie, of course, in the creation of Antony. We may call it so; for, as we saw, he has been cunningly kept, in person and by reference, an ineffectual figure so far. But now both in person and by reference, by preparation, by contrast, Shakespeare brings him to a sudden overwhelming importance.

We have the helter-skelter of the moment after Cæsar's fall; Brutus is the only figure of authority and calm. Old Publius stands trembling and dumb; Antony, that slight man, has fled, and the conspirators seem confounded by their very success. Before, then, they face the Rome they have saved from tyranny, let them make themselves one again, not in false courage—if Rome is ungrateful they must die—but in high principle that fears not death. Let them sign themselves ritual brothers—and in whose blood but Cæsar's?

> Stoop, Romans, stoop,
> And let us bathe our hands in Cæsar's blood
> Up to the elbows, and besmear our swords:
> Then walk we forth, even to the market place,
> And, waving our red weapons o'er our heads,
> Let's all cry, 'Peace, freedom, and liberty!'

We need not doubt Brutus' deep sincerity for a moment.

> Fates, we will know your pleasures.
> That we shall die, we know; 'tis but the time
> And drawing days out, that men stand upon.

This is the man of principle at his noblest. But what else than savage mockery is Casca's

> Why, he that cuts off twenty years of life
> Cuts off so many years of fearing death.

And does Brutus, the rapt ideologue, perceive it? Into the sophistical trap he walks:

> Grant that, and then is death a benefit:
> So are we Cæsar's friends, that have abridg'd
> His time of fearing death.

And he anoints himself devotedly. Then Cassius, febrile, infatuate:

> Stoop, then, and wash. How many ages hence
> Shall this our lofty scene be acted o'er,
> In states unborn and accents yet unknown!

Brutus echoes him as well. And by this last daring and doubly dramatic stroke, Shakespeare reminds us that we are ideal spectators of these men and the event, having vision and prevision too. Comment is forbidden the playwright, but here is the effect of it contrived. For as we look and listen we hear the verdict of the ages echoing. In this imperfect world, it would seem, one can be too high-minded, too patriotic, too virtuous altogether. And then the commonest thing, if it be rooted firm, may trip a man to his ruin. So these exalted gentlemen, led by their philosophic patriot, are stopped on their way—by the arrival of a servant.[12]

This is the play's turning point. And, if but pictorially, could a better be contrived? On the one side the group of triumphant and powerful men; on the other, suddenly appearing, a humble, anonymous messenger.

> Thus, Brutus, did my master bid me kneel;
> Thus did Mark Antony bid me fall down;
> And, being prostrate, thus he bade me say . . .

And so aptly and literally does he represent his master that Brutus, with this chance to test the smooth words apart from their deviser, might, we should suppose, take warning. But it is Brutus who is infatuate now. It is not, as with Cassius, passions that blind him, but principles. He has done murder for an ideal. Not to credit his adversaries, in turn, with the highest motives would be unworthy, would seem sheer hypocrisy. And Antony's message is baited with an uncanny knowledge of the man.

> Brutus is noble, wise, valiant, and honest;
> Cæsar was mighty, bold, royal, and loving:
> Say I love Brutus, and I honour him;
> Say I fear'd Cæsar, honour'd him, and lov'd him.

Wisdom and honesty, valour and love, honour and again honour; Brutus will harp on the very words in his own apology. It is Cassius, with his vengeance fulfilled and his passions gratified, who now sees clear, knowing his Antony as truly as Antony knows his Brutus. His

> misgiving still
> Falls shrewdly to the purpose.

But he lacks authority to lead.

Then follows the revelation of Antony, in his verbal duel with the conspirators; his devoted rhapsody over Cæsar's body; and the swift foresight of the passage with Octavius' servant. It is to be noted that the beginning of the scene in the Forum tags dramatically not to the end of this but to the earlier departure of Brutus and the others. Hence, perhaps, the short opening in verse and Brutus' echoing of his last spoken line,

> Prepare the body, then, and follow us.

with

> Then follow me, and give me audience, friends.

Once he is in the pulpit we have a sharp change to prose.

Editor after editor has condemned Brutus' speech as poor and ineffective, and most of them have then proceeded to justify Shakespeare for making it so. It is certainly not meant to be ineffective, for it attains its end in convincing the crowd. Whether it is poor oratory must be to some extent a matter of taste. Personally, accepting its form as one accepts the musical convention of a fugue, I find that it stirs me deeply. I prefer it to Antony's. It wears better. It is very noble prose. But we must, of course, consider it first as a part of the setting-out of Brutus' character. Nothing—if the speech itself does not—suggests him to us as a poor speaker; nor, at this moment of all others, would he fail himself. But we know the sort of appeal he would, deliberately if not temperamentally, avoid. Shakespeare has been accused, too, of bias against the populace. But is it so? He had no illusions about them. As a popular dramatist he faced their inconstant verdict day by day, and came to write for a better audience than he had. He allows Brutus no illusions, certainly.

> Only be patient till we have appeas'd
> The multitude, beside themselves with fear. . . .

This is the authentic voice of your republican aristocrat, who is at no pains, either, to disguise his disdain.

> Be patient till the last.
> Romans, countrymen and lovers! hear me for my cause; and be silent, that you may hear. . . .

For the tone belies the words; nor is such a rapping on the desk for 'Quiet, please' the obvious way into the affections of the heady crowd. He concedes nothing to their simplicity.

> Censure me in your wisdom, and awake your senses, that you may be the better judge.

But the compliment, one fears, is paid less to them than to his own intellectual pride. It is wasted in any case, if we may judge by the Third and Fourth Citizens:

> Let him be Cæsar.
> Cæsar's better parts
> Shall be crown'd in Brutus.

He has won them; not by what he has said, in spite of it, rather; but by what he is. The dramatic intention, and the part the crowd plays in it, is surely plain. Men in the mass do not think, they feel. They are as biddable as children, and as sensitive to suggestion. Mark Antony is to make it plainer.

Antony has entered, and stands all friendless by Cæsar's bier. Brutus descends, the dialogue shifting from prose to easy verse as he shakes free of the enthusiasm, and departs alone. His austere renouncing of advantage should show us how truly alone.

Antony makes no glib beginning; he protests, indeed, that he has nothing to say. He tries this opening and that, is deprecatory, apologetic.

> The noble Brutus
> Hath told you Cæsar was ambitious;
> If it were so, it was a grievous fault,
> And grievously hath Cæsar answered it.

But he is deftly feeling his way by help of a few platitudes to his true opening, and alert for a first response. He senses one, possibly, upon his

> He was my friend, faithful and just to me. . . .

—for that was a human appeal. But he knows better than to presume on a success; he returns to his praise of the well-bepraised Brutus. He embellishes his tune with two grace notes, one appealing to sentiment, the other to greed. More praise of Brutus, and yet more! But the irony of this will out, and he checks himself. Irony is a tricky weapon with an audience uncertain still. Nor will too much nice talk about honour serve him; that sort of thing leaves men cold. A quick turn gives us

> I speak not to disprove what Brutus spoke,
> But here I am to speak what I do know.

and, to judge by the hammering monosyllables of the last line, he is warming to his work, and feels his hearers warming to him.

One may so analyze the speech throughout and find it a triumph of effective cleverness. The cheapening of the truth, the appeals to passion, the perfect carillon of flattery, cajolery, mockery and pathos, swinging to a magnificent tune, all serve to make it a model of what popular oratory should be. In a school for demagogues its critical analysis might well be an item in every examination paper. That is one view of it. By another, there is nothing in it calculated or false. Antony feels like this; and, on these occasions, he never lets his thoughts belie his feelings, that is all. And he knows, without stopping to think, what the common thought and feeling will be, where reason and sentiment will touch bottom—and if it be a muddy bottom, what matter!—because he is himself, as we said, the common man raised to the highest power. So, once in touch with his audience, he can hardly go wrong.

How easy he makes things for them! No abstract arguments:

> But here's a parchment with the seal of Cæsar;
> I found it in his closet, 'tis his will.[13]

We pass now, however, to a less ingenuous, more ingenious, phase of the achievement. Those—it is strange there should be any—who range themselves with the mob and will see in Antony no more than the plain blunt man of his own painting, have still to account for this slim manipulator of Cæsar's will that Shakespeare paints. It is tempting, no doubt, to make men dance to your tune when the thing is done so easily. When they stand, open-eared and open-mouthed, how resist stuffing them with any folly that comes handy? And as there is no limit, it would seem, to their folly and credulity, greed and baseness, why not turn it all to good account—one's own account? Antony is not the man, at any rate, to

turn aside from such temptation. Is he less of a demagogue that Cæsar's murder is his theme, and vengeance
for it his cause? Does poetic eloquence make demagogy
less vicious—or, by chance, more? Shakespeare's Antony
would not be complete without this juggling with Cæsar's
will.

What so impresses the unlearned as the sight of some
document? He does not mean to read it. They are
Cæsar's heirs. There, he never meant to let that slip!
Trick after trick of the oratorical trade follows. The
provocative appeal to the seething crowd's self-control
tagged to the flattery of their generous hearts, the play
with the mantle, which they 'all do know', that soft touch
of the 'summer's evening' when Cæsar first put it on!
Self-interest well salted with sentiment, what better bait
can there be? Much may be done with a blood-stained
bit of cloth!

> Through this the well-beloved Brutus stabbed;
> And as he pluck'd his cursèd steel away,
> Mark how the blood of Cæsar followed it,
> As rushing out of doors, to be resolved
> If Brutus so unkindly knocked, or no....

If our blood were still cold the simile might sound
ridiculous, but it thrills us now.

> This was the most unkindest cut of all;
> For when the noble Cæsar saw him stab,
> Ingratitude, more strong than traitors' arms,
> Quite vanquished him: then burst his mighty heart;
> And, in his mantle muffling up his face,
> Even at the base of Pompey's statua,
> Which all the while ran blood, great Cæsar fell.

How fine it sounds! How true, therefore, by the standards of popular oratory, it is! There is poetic truth,

certainly, in that ingratitude; and as for Pompey's statue,
if it did not actually run blood, it might well have done.

> O! what a fall was there, my countrymen;
> Then I, and you, and all of us fell down,
> Whilst bloody treason flourished over us.
> O! now you weep, and I perceive you feel
> The dint of pity. . . .

What were Brutus' tributes to their wisdom compared
to this? Antony has won their tears, and has but to seal
his success by showing them the very body of Cæsar,
and to endorse it with

> Good friends, sweet friends, let me not stir you up
> To such a sudden flood of mutiny.
> They that have done this deed are honourable. . . .

for irony is a potent weapon now; and to forbid mutiny
is only to encourage it, the word of itself will do so.

The peroration is masterly, a compendium of excitement. We have again the false restraint from passion,
the now triumphant mockery of those honourable men,
of their wisdom, their good reasons and their private
grief; again, the plain blunt man's warning against such
oratorical snares as the subtle Brutus set; and it is all
rounded off with magnificent rhythm, the recurrent
thought and word flung like a stone from a sling.

> but were I Brutus,
> And Brutus Antony, there were an Antony
> Would ruffle up your spirits, and put a tongue
> In every wound of Cæsar that should move
> The stones of Rome to rise and mutiny.

And to what end? To the routing of the conspirators
from Rome, truly. A good counterstroke. But the first
victim of Antony's eloquence, as Shakespeare takes care

to show us, is the wretched Cinna the poet, who has had nothing to do with Cæsar's murder at all.[14] The mob tear him limb from limb, as children tear a rag doll. Nor does knowledge of his innocence hinder them.

> Truly, my name is Cinna.
> Tear him to pieces, he's a conspirator.
> I am Cinna, the poet, I am Cinna the poet.
> Tear him for his bad verses, tear him for his bad verses.
> I am not Cinna the conspirator.
> It is no matter, his name's Cinna; pluck but his name out of his heart, and turn him going.

Well, we have had Antony's fine oratory; and we may have been, and should have been, stirred by it. But if we have not at the same time watched him, and ourselves, with a discerning eye, and listened as well with a keener ear, the fault is none of Shakespeare's. He draws no moral, does not wordily balance the merits of this cause against that. He is content to compose for the core of his play, with an artist's enjoyment, with an artist's conscience, in getting the balance true, this ironic picture; and, finally, to set against the high tragedy of the murder of Cæsar a poor poetaster's wanton slaughter.

The beginning of the fourth act sets against the calculations of the conspirators the arithmetic of the new masters of Rome.

> These many then shall die; their names are pricked.

It is an admirably done scene, of but fifty lines all told, giving an actor, with just twenty-two words, material for Lepidus (the feat would seem impossible, but Shakespeare manages it; and so can an actor, rightly chosen and given scope), giving us Octavius, showing us yet another Antony, and outlining the complete gospel of political success. Brutus and Cassius, its finish informs

us, are levying powers. We are shown them straightway
at the next scene's beginning, and from now to the play's
end its action runs a straight road.

> *Drum. Enter Brutus. . . .*

The philosopher has turned general. He is graver, more
austere than ever.

> Your master, Pindarus,
> In his own change, or by ill officers,
> Hath given me some worthy cause to wish
> Things done undone. . . .

But he says it as one who would say that nothing, be it
big or little, can ever be undone. We hear a *Low march
within,* congruous accompaniment to the somber voice.
It heralds Cassius.

> *Enter Cassius and his Powers.*
> CASSIUS.   Stand, ho!
> BRUTUS.   Stand, ho!
> 1ST SOLDIER. Stand!
> 2ND SOLDIER. Stand!
> 3RD SOLDIER. Stand!

The voices echo back, the drumbeats cease, the armed
men face each other, silent a moment.[15]

This long scene—the play's longest—thus begun, is
dominated by Brutus and attuned in the main to his
mood. Now the mood of the good man in adversity may
well make for monotony and gloom; but Shakespeare is
alert to avoid this, and so must producer and actors be.
We have the emotional elaboration of the quarrel, the
eccentric interlude of the poet as preparation for the
sudden drop to the deep still note struck by the revelation of Portia's death; next comes the steady talk of
fighting plans (note the smooth verse), then the little stir

with which the council breaks up and the simple prep-
arations for the night. Varro and Claudius are brought
in, so that their sleep, as well as the boy's, may throw
the calm, wakeful figure of Brutus into relief. The tune
and its lapsing brings a hush, we can almost hear the
leaves of the book rustle as they are turned. Then the
ghost appears; the tense few moments of its presence
have been well prepared. The scene's swift ending is
good stagecraft too. Lucius' protesting treble, the deeper
voices of the soldiers all confused with sleep, the disson-
ance and sharp interchange break and disperse the
ominous spell for Brutus and for us. And the last words
look forward.[16]

The last act of *Julius Cæsar* has been most inconsider-
ately depreciated. Nothing, certainly, will make it effective upon the modern 'realistic' stage, but we can hardly
blame Shakespeare for that. He writes within the conventions of his own theatre, and he here takes the fullest
advantage of them. He begins by bringing the rival
armies, led by their generals, face to face.

> *Enter Octavius, Antony and their army....*
> *Drum. Enter Brutus, Cassius and their army.*

BRUTUS. They stand, and would have parley.
CASSIUS. Stand fast, Titinius; we must out and talk.
OCTAVIUS. Mark Antony, shall we give sign of battle?
ANTONY. No, Cæsar, we will answer on their charge.
　Make forth; the generals would have some words .

This to the Elizabethans was a commonplace of stagecraft. Before scenery which paints realistically some
defined locality, it must needs look absurd. But, the
simpler convention accepted, Shakespeare sets for his
audience a wider and more significant scene than any
the scenic theatre can compass. And, confronting the

fighters, he states the theme, so to speak, of the play's last event, and gives it value, importance and dignity.

The whole act is constructed with great skill, each detail has its purpose and effect. But we must dismiss, even from our memories if possible, the *Scene ii, The same, the Field of Battle*; and *Scene iii, Another Part of the Field*, of the editors. What happens to begin with is this. Antony, Octavius and their powers departed, the talk between Brutus and Cassius over—it is (for us) their third and last, and a chill quiet talk; they feel they are under the shadow of defeat—the stage is left empty. Then the silence is broken by the clattering *Alarum*, the symbol of a battle begun. Then back comes Brutus, but a very different Brutus.

> Ride, ride, Messala, ride, and give these bills
> Unto the legions on the other side.

Now a *Loud alarum*, which his voice must drown.

> Let them set on at once, for I perceive
> But cold demeanour in Octavius' wing,
> And sudden push gives them the overthrow.
> Ride, ride, Messala: let them all come down.

And he is gone as he came. In its sharp contrast it is a stirring passage, which restores to Brutus whatever dominance he may have lost. But it cannot be achieved if tension is relaxed and attention dissipated by the shifting of scenery, or by any superfluous embroidering of the action.

Remark further that to follow the course of the battle an audience must listen keenly, and they must be able to concentrate their minds on the speakers. When the defeat of Cassius is imminent, when Titinius tells him:

> O Cassius! Brutus gave the word too early;
> Who, having some advantage on Octavius,

> Took it too eagerly: his soldiers fell to spoil,
> Whilst we by Antony are all enclos'd.

the situation is made clear enough. But if we do not master it at this moment, the rest of the scene and its drama will go for next to nothing.

Now we have Cassius grasping the ensign he has seized from the coward who was running away with it (and, being Cassius, not content with that, he has killed the man), the very ensign the birds of ill omen had hovered over; and he makes as if to plant it defiantly, conspicuously in the ground.

> This hill is far enough.

His death is of a piece with his whole reckless life. He kills himself because he will not wait another minute to verify the tale his bondman tells him of Titinius' capture. He ends passionately and desperately—but still grasping his standard. Even at this moment he is as harsh to Pindarus as Brutus is gentle to his boy Lucius and the bondman who serves him:

> Come hither, sirrah:
> In Parthia did I take thee prisoner;
> And then I swore thee, saving of thy life,
> That whatsoever I did bid thee do,
> Thou shouldst attempt it.

His last words are as bare and ruthless.

> Cæsar, thou art reveng'd,
> Even with the sword that kill'd thee.

Pindarus' four lines that follow may seem frigid and formal. But we need a breathing-space before we face the tragically ironic return of Titinius radiant with good news. The stagecraft of this entrance, as of others like it, belongs, we must (yet again) remember, to the Elizabethan theatre, with its doors at the back, and its distance for an actor to advance, attention full on him. Entrance from the wing of a conventional scenic stage will be quite another matter.

> MESSALA. It is but change, Titinius; for Octavius
>   Is overthrown by noble Brutus' power,
>   As Cassius' legions are by Antony.
> TITINIUS. These tidings will well comfort Cassius.
> MESSALA. Where did you leave him?
> TITINIUS.   All disconsolate,
>   With Pindarus his bondman, on this hill.
> MESSALA. Is that not he that lies along the ground?
> TITINIUS. He lies not like the living. O my heart!
> MESSALA. Is not that he?
> TITINIUS.   No, this was he, Messala,
>   But Cassius is no more.

Stage direction is embodied in dialogue. We have the decelerated arrival telling of relief from strain, the glance around the seemingly empty place; then the sudden swift single-syllabled line and its repetition, Titinius' dart forward, Messala's graver question, the dire finality of the answer.

We come to Titinius' death; and it is a legitimate query why, with two suicides to provide for, Shakespeare burdened himself with this third. The episode itself may have attracted him; the soldier crowning his dead chief with the garland of victory; then, as the innocent cause of his death, set not to survive it.[17] The death speech is fine, and the questioning sentences that begin it whip it to great poignancy. But neither here nor anywhere, we must admit, does Shakespeare show full understanding of the 'Roman's part' and the strange faith that let him play it. His Romans go to their deaths stoically enough, but a little stockily too. Hamlet, later, will find the question arguable, and Macbeth will think a man a fool not to die fighting. Brutus and Cassius and Titinius, it is true, could hardly be made to argue the point here. But there is an abruptness and a sameness, and a certain emptiness, in the manner of these endings.

Another and technically a stronger reason for adding Titinius to the suicides, is that it is above all important Brutus' death should not come as an anticlimax to Cassius'. This episode helps provide against that danger, and the next scene makes escape from it sure.

The bodies are carried out in procession with due dignity, and again the effect of the empty stage keys us to expectancy. Then

Alarum. Enter Brutus, Messala, Cato, Lucilius and Flavius.
Enter soldiers and fight.

It is a noisy mêlée; so confused that, though we hear the voices of the leaders from its midst, Brutus disappears unnoticed. The scene has its touch of romance in young Cato's death, its dash of intrigue in Lucilius' trick. If these things are given value in performance, they knot up effectively the weakening continuity of theme, which, by its slacking, would leave the death of Brutus and the play's end a fag end instead of a full close.

Yet the effects of the last scene are in themselves most carefully elaborated. Hard upon the clattering excitement of the fight, and the flattering magnanimity of the triumphant Antony, comes into sight this little group of beaten and exhausted men, the torchlight flickering on their faces.[18]

BRUTUS. Come, poor remains of friends, rest on this rock.
CLITUS. Statilius show'd the torch-light; but, my lord,
   He came not back: he is or ta'en or slain.

> BRUTUS. Sit thee down, Clitus: slaying is the word;
> It is a deed in fashion. . . .

They throw themselves down hopelessly; to wait—for what!—and to brood in a silence which Brutus hardly breaks by his whisper, first to Clitus, next to Dardanius. Then he paces apart while the two watch him and themselves whisper of the dreadful demand he made. He calls on Volumnius next, to find in him, not hope, only the instinctive human reluctance to admit an end. But his own end—and he knows and desires it—is here. Threatening low alarums vibrate beneath his calm, colourless speech. His followers cry to him to save himself, and a like cry from far off pierces that still insistent alarum, and they echo it again. Well, these men have life and purpose left in them; let them go. He praises and humours their loyalty. But, at his command, they leave him. The end is very near.

But Shakespeare himself is not yet at the end of his resources, nor of his constant care to weave the action in a living texture, to give the least of its figures life. What, till this moment, do we know about Strato? He makes his first appearance in the battle; he is Brutus' body-servant, it seems. A thick-skinned sort of fellow; while the others counted the cost of their ruin, he had fallen asleep. Twelve lines or so (he himself speaks just seven) not only make a living figure of him but keep Brutus self-enlightening to the last. For the very last note struck out of this stoic, whose high principles could not stop short of murder, is one of gentleness.

> BRUTUS. I prithee, Strato, stay thou by thy lord:
> Thou art a fellow of a good respect;
> Thy life hath had some smatch of honour in it:
> Hold then my sword, and turn away thy face,
> While I do run upon it. Wilt thou, Strato?

STRATO. Give me your hand first: fare you well, my lord.
BRUTUS. Farewell, good Strato. . . .

The man's demand for a handshake, the master's response
to it;—how much of Shakespeare's greatness lies in these
little things, and in the love of his art that never found
them too little for his care! Then Brutus closes his account.

> Cæsar, now be still:
> I kill'd not thee with half so good a will.

In silence on both sides the thing is done. Nor does
Strato stir while the loud alarum and retreat are
sounded; he does not even turn at the conquerors'
approach—Antony, Octavius and the already reconciled
Messala and Lucilius, who only see by the light of the
torches this solitary figure standing there.

Nor have we even yet reached the play's formal close,
the ceremonial lifting of the body, the apostrophe to the
dead, and that turning towards the living future which
the conditions of the Elizabethan stage inevitably and
happily prescribed. Chief place is given here, as we have
noted, to Octavius, Cæsar's heir and—if Shakespeare
may have had it in mind—the conqueror-to-be of his
fellow-conqueror. But we have first a bitter-sweet exchange between Strato and Messala. They—and they
know it—are commoner clay than their master who lies
here; no vain heroism for them. Next Antony speaks,
and makes sportsmanlike amends to his dead enemy.

The play is a masterpiece of Elizabethan stagecraft,
and the last act, from this point of view, especially
remarkable; but only by close analysis can its technical
virtues be made plain. Within the powerful ease of its
larger rhythm, the constant, varied ebb and flow and
interplay of purpose, character and event give it richness
of dramatic life, and us the sense of its lifelikeness.

Staging and Costume

No difficulties arise—why should they?—in fitting the play to such a stage as we suppose Shakespeare's at the Globe to have been; at most a few questions must be answered as to the use of the inner stage for this scene or that. Further, the resources of this stage, its adapting of space and time to the playwright's convenience, are so fully exploited that the producer who means to use another had better be very careful he does not lose more than he gains.

Act I can be played wholly on the main stage.

Act II. *Enter Brutus in his Orchard*, says the Folio. This looks like a discovery upon the inner stage. There will certainly be the dramatic effect of contrast, after the feverish excursions through the night of storm, in our seeing Brutus, a chief subject of them, sitting in the contained quiet of his garden. The opening speech, by which, as a rule, Shakespeare paints us the aspect of his scene if he wants to, gives it its tone and in its interspersed silences both the solitary man and the stillness after the storm:

> What, Lucius! ho!
> I cannot, by the progress of the stars,
> Give guess how near to day. Lucius, I say!
> I would it were my fault to sleep so soundly.
> When, Lucius, when! Awake, I say! what, Lucius!

Lucius may enter directly upon the inner stage. Brutus might speak his first soliloquy still sitting there. It is possible that at the Globe he did not, the actor there may have needed a better point of vantage for such an intimately reflective passage.[19] The knocking would almost certainly be heard beyond one of the main-stage doors, through which the conspirators would come, for the scene's general action must be upon the main stage without a doubt. For the scene which follows the traverse must, one would suppose, be closed, to hide whatever properties suggested Brutus' garden. But *Enter Cæsar in his nightgown*, even though he enter upon the main stage, will sufficiently suggest an interior. And the main stage will serve for the rest of the second act.

We should note the space-freedom Shakespeare assumes. 'Here will I stand', says Artemidorus, 'till Cæsar pass along'; but, speaking five lines more, he goes off, to reappear with the crowd that follows Cæsar. And Act III begins with a most significant instance of it. The inner stage is disclosed and Cæsar's 'state' is set there. Cæsar, the conspirators, the Senators and the populace enter upon the main stage. Cassius speaks to Artemidorus:

> What! urge you your petitions in the street?
> Come to the Capitol.

Eighteen lines later we have

CÆSAR.   Are we all ready? what is now amiss
   That Cæsar and his Senate must redress?
METELLUS. Most high, most mighty, and most puissant Cæsar,
   Metellus Cimber throws before thy seat
   An humble heart—

Nothing more complicated has occurred than Cæsar and the Senators taking their places, while the crowd disperses and the conspirators regroup themselves, so that the 'state' becomes the centre of attraction—and we are in the Senate House. Later, Cæsar must fall and lie dead in a most conspicuous position upon the main stage; still later provision must be made—as it is—for removing the body.

For the following scene the traverse is closed and the upper stage is used for the pulpit. Moreover, the dialogue tells us, to a second or so, the time it takes to ascend and come down.

The first scene of Act IV might, but need not, be played in relation to the inner stage.[20] The second and third scenes, which are not divided in the Folio—which are indeed conspicuously left undivided there—present us with another significant instance of space-freedom, and of Shakespeare's ready use of the conventions which belong to it.[21] We have

Enter Brutus, Lucilius and the Army. . . .

The editors cannot leave this alone. '*The Army*' becomes '*and soldiers*'.[22] This falsifies Shakespeare's intention. By '*the Army*' he does not mean a few casual soldiers, he means the integral group of followers, in some uniform possibly, and with banner, drum and trumpet, which in Elizabethan stage convention personified and symbolized an army entire. Later, after a *Low march within* comes

Enter Cassius and his Powers.

And much the same thing is meant. The effect to be gained is of the spaciousness and order of armies in the field in contrast with that chaos of the market place; and it is as important as an explanatory scene would be.

And what really occurs where modern editors mark a change of scene?

> BRUTUS. Let us not wrangle: bid them move away;
>   Then in my tent, Cassius, enlarge your griefs,
>   And I will give you audience.
> CASSIUS.   Pindarus,
>   Bid our commanders lead their charges off
>   A little from this ground.

BRUTUS. Lucius, do you the like; and let no man
    Come to our tent till we have done our conference.

> *Exeunt. Manet Brutus and Cassius.*

Then, without more ado, with no slackening of tension
nor waste of this excellently ominous preparation, the
intimate wrangle begins. The stagecraft is plain enough.
The symbolized armies, with their banners and drums,
go off; and either the traverse is now drawn, disclosing
the tent furniture, in which case Brutus and Cassius have
but to place themselves in relation to it for the scene to
be effectively changed; or it is as possible that the
traverse has been open from the beginning and that the
removal of the 'armies' and the reorientation of the chief
actors were felt to be change enough. This would repeat
the mechanics of the Senate House scene (but it would,
of course, forbid an immediately previous use of the
inner stage for Antony and Octavius).

We come to Act V, which must be envisaged as a
whole. The locality is a battlefield. We have still the
symbolical armies. The scenes are divided by alarums.
The conventions, in fact, are all accepted. The upper
stage is used, for a moment, as the high point of a hill.

> Go, Pindarus, get higher on that hill,

says Cassius, and six lines later the direction reads:

> *Pindarus above.*

The only sign of use of the inner stage is for the scene
beginning,

> BRUTUS. Come, poor remains of friends, rest on this rock.

Brutus and his friends may need something better to sit
upon than the floor. It need be no realistic rock, for a
while back when Cassius said,

This hill is far enough.

there certainly was no hill. On the other hand, if you require some things to sit on it is as easy to make them look like rocks as anything else. The rock or rocks, in that case, would have to be set upon the inner stage. A further indication of its use is the mention of torches, for these would show up better in its comparative shade.

The question of costume raises difficulties. Shakespeare, by convention, dressed his Romans more or less in Elizabethan clothes. To those of the chief characters (for whom this could be afforded) some definitely exotic touches have been added.[23] Nationality, we know, was, at times, pointed by costume. So, possibly, was period; but not, one suspects, with any consistency, not, for a certainty, with any historical accuracy. In this text, at any rate, while there are no direct indications of 'Roman habitings', there are a round dozen of references to the Elizabethan. Therefore we cannot simply ignore Shakespeare's convention in favour of our own, which pictures the ancient Roman, bare-headed, clean-shaven and wrapped in a toga.[24] But then, neither can we very easily and altogether ignore our own. The questions of costume and scenery differ in this: whatever the background, if one is kept conscious of it once the play's acting is under way, it is a bad background; but the look of the actors is of constant importance. We are in this dilemma, then. Cæsar, we hear, plucks ope his doublet; the conspirators' hats are plucked about their ears; Brutus walks unbraced and turns down the leaf of a book which he keeps in the pocket of his gown. Do these seem trivial things? Nothing in a play is trivial which bears upon the immediate credibility of the action. The theatre is a game of make-believe, and the rules of any game may be varied by use and acceptance, but mere contrariness is tiresome.

An actor may point into vacancy and fill it by description, and we shall be at one with him; but to wear a toga, and call it a doublet, will be distracting. And, apart from direct verbal contradictions, there are passages enough whose full effect must remain one with the picture Shakespeare made of them. The boy Lucius asleep over his lute; who ever can have realized that episode in its exact and delicate detail and want to transform and botch it? Yet it must be confessed that a Cæsar in doublet and hose may offend and will undoubtedly distract us.

The difficulty must, I suggest, be met by compromise, in which we can find some positive advantage too. We are not concerned with the accuracy of our own picturing of Rome, but to reconcile two dramatic conventions. It goes without saying that the nearer we can in general come to Shakespeare's point of view the better. But for a particular gain, has not the vulgar modern conception of Rome, nourished on Latin lessons and the classic school of painting, become rather frigid? Are not our noble Romans, flinging their togas gracefully about them, slow-moving, consciously dignified, speaking with studied oratory and all past middle age, rather too like a schoolboy's vision of a congress of headmasters? Compare them with the high-mettled, quick-tongued crew of politicians and fighters that Shakespeare imagines; and if it comes to accuracy, has he not more the right of it than we, even though his Cæsar be dressed in doublet and hose? So let the designer at least provide an escape from this cold classicism, which belongs neither to the true Rome nor to the play he has to interpret. His way can be the way of all compromise. What need each side insist on? The figure of Brutus must not make a modern audience think all the time of Shakespeare himself, but where the gain to Shakespeare that it should? On the other hand, whatever has been woven, even casually, into the fabric of the play, we must somehow manage to respect. If we change, we must not falsify.

The methods of the Masque and the way of Renaissance painters with classical subjects give us the hint we need. Whether from taste or lack of information, when it came to picturing Greeks and Romans they were for fancy dress; a mixture, as a rule, of helmet, cuirass, trunk hose, stockings and sandals, like nothing that ever was worn, but very wearable and delightful to look at. Women's dresses seem to have been manipulated less easily; perhaps the wearers were not so amenable, or so tolerant of the outrage upon fashion.[25] But even here something of the sort is managed. And something of the sort, with emphasis upon this period or that, according to his judgment, will get our designer out of his difficulty. Shakespeare's own consent, so to speak, to such a compromise can be determined, for the tests are all to hand before ever the play is acted. Upon the tacit consent of an audience one can only speculate. But the problem with an audience in this as in other things is less to satisfy their opinion, if they have one, than to release them from its burden for the fuller, the unselfconscious, enjoyment of the play. *Julius Cæsar*! They may come expecting the familiarized figures set against some popular picture-book background of Rome. For good reasons given they cannot have this. The designer must overreach them. He must appeal, that is to say, past expectation and opinion, to their readiness to be pleased and convinced; and there are no rules by which that can be forecast. But this much law can be laid down. He must first be sure that his work will fuse with Shakespeare's. What Shakespeare's purposes will not accept, he must reject. For the rest, he may be bold or cautious as it suits him. He had better be simple. If he can so picture the play to himself that nothing in the picture raises any thought but of the play, he will probably not go far wrong.

The Music

ONLY one difficulty presents itself; we are given no text for the *Music and a Song* of Act IV, Scene iii. Custom prescribes the use of

> Orpheus with his lute made trees. . . .

from *Henry VIII*, and this may well be allowed. Mr Richmond Noble in his *Shakespeare's Use of Song* suggests that the stage direction in the Folio may be a later interpolation and that no song is called for, only the playing of an air. This he would presumably justify by Brutus'

> Canst thou hold up thy heavy eyes awhile,
> And touch thy instrument a strain or two?

But a song would be more usual, a lute solo not very audible in a public theatre, and the evidence of the Folio is not negligible.[26] This apart, we have only to give careful attention to the sennets, flourishes, drums, and marches, alarums, low alarums and retreats, which find place throughout the play, for they have each a particular purpose.

A Stumbling Block in the Text

THE text, as the first Folio gives it us, is an exceptionally clean one and I do not examine its few minor difficulties here. There is, however, one serious stumbling block in Act IV. What are we to make of the duplicate revelation of Portia's death? The question has, of course, been argued high and low and round about, and weighty opinion will be found set out in the Furness Variorum. The weightier the worse, one is driven to complain. For surely it is clear that a mere corruption of text is involved, not the degeneracy of Brutus' character. Shakespeare may have fumbled a little at this point. But that his final intention was to give us a Brutus wantonly 'showing off' to Messala or indulging at this moment in a supersubtle defence of his grief, I would take leave to dispute against the weightiest opinion in the world. One must, however, suggest some explanation; and here is mine. It is not provably correct, but I suggest that corrections of text are not provable. The vagaries of a playwright's mind may be guessed at, they can never be brought within the four corners of a system and so tested.

My guess is that Shakespeare originally wrote this, or something like it:

BRUTUS. Lucius, a bowl of wine.
CASSIUS. I did not think you could have been so angry.[27]
       Enter boy with wine, and tapers.
BRUTUS. In this I bury all unkindness, Cassius. . . .

And so on as the text now stands, omitting, however, both

CASSIUS. Portia, art thou gone?
BRUTUS. No more, I pray you.

and (possibly)

CASSIUS. Cicero one?
MESSALA. Cicero is dead, and by that order of proscription.

These have something the air of additions, designed to keep Cassius active in the scene; and the first, of course, involves his knowledge of Portia's death. By this text Brutus first hears the news from Messala, and he exhibits a correct stoicism.[28] Then Shakespeare found that this made his hero not so much stoical as wooden, so he threw the disclosure back into closer conjunction with the quarrel and made it an immediate, and sharply contrasted, sequel to the eccentric-comic interruption by the poet. The passage here has all the air of a thing done at a breath, and by a man who had taken a fresh breath for it too. Whether or no thereafter he cut Messala's disclosure I do not feel positive.[29] He may have thought there was now a double effect to be gained (the original one had not been perhaps so bad, it had only not been good enough); and, in performance, there is an arbitrary sort of effect in the passage as it stands. It is quite likely that, patching at the thing, he did not see to what subtle reflections upon Brutus' character the new combination would give rise (so seldom apparently did he consider the troubles of his future editors!). I hope that he made the cut. I think on the whole that he did. I am sure that he should have done; and I recommend the producer of today to make it, and by no means to involve his Brutus in that incidental lie, nor his character in the even more objectionable subtleties of an escape from it.

Notes

1 It may well be, however, that with *Henry V* Shakespeare had surmised a patriot audience's instinct to demand for their hero trappings that a legendary foreigner like Cæsar could do well enough without.

2 Cf. p. 62 also.

3   Even by the rule of that philosophy
         By which I did blame Cato ...

   Furness collects four full pages of notes endeavouring to discover exactly what Brutus does mean.

4 The omission of his name among the entrants may, of course, be a mere slip. In that case it is his silence throughout the

scene which will be remarkable—which the actors of Cæsar and Cassius, at any rate, could hardly help making so.

5 As R.G. Moulton demonstrates in an admirable passage in *Shakespeare as Dramatic Artist.*

6 How many modern actors upon their picture stage, with its curtain to close a scene for them pat upon some triumphant top note, have brought this one to its end twenty lines earlier upon the familiar, tremendous, breathless apostrophe (did Shakespeare ever pen such another sentence?) that begins,

> Woe to the hand that shed this costly blood!
> Over thy wounds now do I prophesy . . .

But to how untimely an end! The mechanism of Shakespeare's theatre forbade such effects. Cæsar's body is lying on the main stage, and must be removed, and it will take at least two people to carry it. Here is one reason for the arrival of Octavius' servant. But as ever with Shakespeare, and with any artist worth his salt, limitation is turned to advantage. If dead Cæsar is to be the mainspring of the play's further action, what more forceful way could be found of making this plain than, for a finish to the scene, to state the new theme of Octavius' coming, Cæsar's kin and successor?

7 See p. 82.

8 *Julius Cæsar* begins the cycle of Shakespeare's greater plays, and *Antony and Cleopatra* ends it. The later relations of Octavius and Antony are implicit in this little scene. The realist, losing grip, will find himself 'out-realized' by his pupil.

9 But this might often be as true, if in another degree, of the individual scene.

10 Here, incidentally, is an instance of an effect made for its own sake and in the confidence that no awkward questions will be asked. The immediate suggestion is that Brutus and Ligarius go straight to the conspirators, thence with them to Cæsar and the Senate House. It is left mere suggestion and not further defined, for Portia has to be told of the conspiracy 'by and by', and, when we next see her, the suggestion—still mere suggestion—is that she has been told. But Shakespeare

knows that no questions will be asked as long as the effects are spaced out, if distractions intervene and positive contradiction is avoided.

11 Unless every clearance of the stage is to mark a division of scenes, they are, of course, but one. No particular change of location is implied. Upon the question of the act-division here, see also page 68.

12 For an excellent analysis of this passage see MacCullum's *Shakespeare's Roman Plays*, quoted by Furness. And for the effect of the servant's entrance see, as before noted, R. G. Moulton.

13 And later, he will propose to his colleagues Octavius and Lepidus that they all three consider

How to cut off some charge in legacies.

14 A scene which the average modern producer takes great care to cut.

15 The Chorus in *Henry V* could not apologize enough for the theatre's failure to show armies in being. But by a little music, this cunning of speech and action, and a bold acceptance of convention, these 'ciphers to this great account' can be made to work well enough upon the 'imaginary forces' of the audience.

16 'Sleep again, Lucius', would point, if nothing else did, to the drawing-together of the curtains of the inner stage upon the scene. Where Varro and Claudius have been lying is a question. They enter, of course, upon the main stage. Brutus apparently points to the inner stage with 'Lie in my tent and sleep'. They offer to keep watch where they are, *i.e.* by the door. I am inclined to think that they lie down there, too. This would not only make the business with the ghost better, but it would bring the scene's final piece of action upon the centre stage and give it breadth and importance.

17 Shakespeare finds this more clearly put in Plutarch than he leaves it in the play.

18 It has been held (I do not stress the point) that Elizabethan outdoor performances were timed to end near twilight. In that case the torchlight would prove doubly effective here.

19 I write this very much under correction. But I believe that only experiment will tell us what could and could not be made effective upon the inner and upper stages at the Globe.

20 I think that scenes were more often played 'in relation to' the inner stage than consistently within its boundaries; that is to say, the actors, having gained the effect of a discovery, would be apt to advance upon the main stage, where their movements would be less cramped, where they would be in closer touch with the audience and certainly in a better position to hold an unruly audience. I see this happening in the scene in Brutus' garden, and possibly in this scene. There are signs of such a treatment, too, of the scene in Brutus' tent. When he asks Lucius, 'Where is thy instrument?' 'Here in the tent' is the answer, not a simple 'I have it here.' When he calls in Varro and Claudius, he says, 'I pray you, sirs, lie in my tent and sleep.' It sounds very much like people upon the main stage indicating the inner stage with a gesture. Certain things, the study of the map, the playing of the lute, the reading by the taper's light, show, of course, the use of furniture. This would probably be set and left upon the inner stage, though it would be advantageous to have it placed as near the traverse-line as possible, and actors, using it, would be constantly passing the line. And, speaking generally, one need not suppose that the Elizabethan actor ever saw the division between inner stage and main stage as a fixed boundary, nor that the Elizabethan audience had cultivated such a sense of locality that they questioned its crossing and recrossing or even asked themselves at certain ambiguous moments where exactly the characters were meant to be. The main effect and its dramatic purpose were reckoned with; whatever assisted this was allowed.

21 The play in the Folio (and there are no Quartos) is one of those which start bravely with *Actus Primus, Scæna Prima* and then pay no further attention to scene-division at all. I refer in my enumeration of scenes to the current modern editions, which are, however, in this particular most misleading to the student of the Elizabethan stage and of Shakespeare the dramatist.

22   Capel did no worse than change it to '*Forces*'.

23   See the Henry Peacham illustration to *Titus Andronicus*, repro-
     duced in Chambers' *Shakespearean Gleanings* and elsewhere.

24   Whether our picture is a true one is beside the point. Quite
     possibly the Roman Senate assembled did *not* look like the
     cooling-room of a Turkish bath.

25   Women appeared in the Masques, though not in the publicly
     given plays.

26   Mr Richmond Noble also says that he has recommended the
     use of 'Weep ye no more, sad fountains', from Dowland's
     Third Book of Airs. It is difficult not to recommend such an
     entirely beautiful song when any opportunity occurs. But the
     words of 'Orpheus with his lute' are very appropriate; they
     could, indeed, be made a pertinent enough illustration of
     Shakespeare's use of song.

27   This line of Cassius might be a later addition.

28   Cassius' 'I have as much of this in art as you' does not tell
     against this, for 'art' does not of course mean anything like
     'artfulness'.

29   I now feel positive that he did (1945).

Notes

Notes